e Clarendor

Developments in

Sport, Leisure & Tourism

during the 20th century

Phil Star

PRIFYSGOL
ABERYSTWYTH

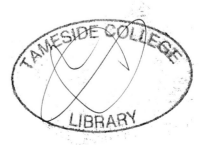

Published by CAA, Aberystwyth University, Gogerddan Mansion, Aberystwyth, Ceredigion, SY23 3EB (www.aber.ac.uk/caa)
Sponsored by the Welsh Government

ISBN: 978-1-84521-439-5

Edited by: Lynwen Rees Jones
Designed by: Richard Huw Pritchard
Printed by: Cambrian Printers

The publisher would like to thank the following for permission to reproduce copyright materials:

Photo credits
p1 Lord Price Collection (*1*), Patrick Brennan (*2*), Popperfoto (*3*), Getty Images(*4-6*); **p2** Lord Price Collection; **p3** Bob Thomas/Popperfoto; **p4** Wrexham County Borough Council; **p6** *t* Lord Price Collection, *b* Getty Images; **p7** *t* Getty Images, *b* Alan George; **p8** *t* Cardiff Council Library Service, *b* Lord Price Collection; **p10** *t* Lizzie Bramlett, *b* Patrick Brennan/donmouth; **p12** Getty Images; **p15** Getty Images; **p16** Getty Images; **p17** Getty Images, (*1, 6*), Sporting Heroes (*2-5*); **p18** *l* State Library of South Australia, *r* The Granger Collection/TopFoto; **p19** *t* Print Collector/ HIP/TopFoto, *b* George Herringshaw/Sporting Heroes; **p20** *l* Soccerbilia; **p23** *t* PA Photos/TopFoto, *b* British Pathé; **p26** *t, c* Getty Images, *b* George Herringshaw/Sporting Heroes; **p27** *t* George Herringshaw/Sporting Heroes, *c* Ed Lacey/Sporting Heroes, *b* Jamie Squire/Getty Images; **p28** *t* George Herringshaw/Sporting Heroes, *b* AFP/Getty Images; **p31** *t* Sporting Heroes (*1, 6*), Getty Images (*2, 3*), TopFoto (*4, 5*); **p32** Royal Commission on the Ancient and Historical Monuments of Wales; **p34** iStock; **p35** AFP/Getty Images; **p37** George Herringshaw/Sporting Heroes; **p38** *t* Urdd Gobaith Cymru, *b* Young Farmers Club Wales; **p39** Huw Evans Picture Agency; **p40** George Herringshaw/Sporting Heroes; **p43** Elen Jones; **p44** Richard Huw Pritchard; **p45** *t* Topham Picturepoint/TopFoto, *b* Popperfoto/Getty Images; **p46** *t* TopFoto, *b* Jan Pitman/Getty Images; **p48** George Herringshaw/Sporting Heroes; **p51** John Gichigi/Getty Images; **p53** National Library of Wales (*1, 4*), Getty Images (*2, 3, 6*), Trustees of the Newbridge Memo (*5*); **p54** John Thomas Collection/ National Library of Wales; **p55** *t* National Library of Wales, *b* Trustees of the Newbridge Memo; **p57** Buyenlarge/Getty Images; **p58** National Library of Wales; **p60** Getty Images; **p61** Caerphilly County Borough Museums and Heritage Service; **p62** Getty Images; **p63** Getty Images; **p67** Getty Images (*1, 2*), TopFoto (*3, 5*), Sain (Records) Ltd (*4*), Lambeth Archives (*6*); **p68** ClassicStock/TopFoto; **p71** *l* Radio Times, *r* Getty Images; **p72** Getty Images; **p73** Lambeth Archives; **p75** Topham Picturepoint/ TopFoto; **p77** loti.com; **p78** *t* Mirrorpix, *b* Sain (Records) Ltd; **p79** TopFoto; **p81** Mirrorpix; **p85** *l-r* Mercury Press Agency, Mirrorpix, CartoonStock, Getty Images, Abbey Home Media Group, TopFoto; **p86** Mirrorpix; **p87** Time & Life Pictures/Getty Images; **p90** *t* Mercury Press Agency, *b* Peter Cade/Getty Images; **p91** *t* Abbey Home Media Group, *b* CartoonStock; **p93** Richard Huw Pritchard; **p94** *t* TopFoto, *b* CartoonStock; **p99** Getty Images (*1-3, 5*), Blaenau Gwent County Council (*4*), TopFoto (*6*); **p100** *t* Ullsteinbild/TopFoto, *b* Geoff Felix Archive; **p101** SSPL via Getty Images; **p102** SSPL via Getty Images; **p103** *l* Blaenau Gwent County Council, *r* SSPL via Getty Images; **p104** Popperfoto/ Getty Images; **p109** *l-r* Aberdareonline, Lord Price Collection, English Heritage, TopFoto, Photolibrary Wales, Britain's National Parks; **p110** Aberdareonline; **p112** *t* BygoneButlins, *b* TopFoto; **p114** Southlakes; **p115** *l* Britain's National Parks, *r* Photolibrary Wales, *b* English Heritage/ HIP/TopFoto; **p116** Lord Price Collection; **p119** *l-r* Llancaiach Fawr/Caerphilly CBC, TopFoto, Visit Wales Image Centre, Clwyd Leisure, Getty Images, Photo Library Wales; **p120** Realbenidorm; **p121** Getty Images; **p122** CartoonStock; **p124** *t* Clwyd Leisure, *b* Photo Library Wales; **p125** *t* Topham Picturepoint/TopFoto, *c* Visit Wales Image Centre, *b* Llancaiach Fawr/Caerphilly CBC; **p127** AFP/Getty Images; **p130** TopFoto/HIP; **p131** Topham Picturepoint/TopFoto.

Acknowledgements
p3 Source A: W.H.Davies, *The Right Place, the Right Time* (1972); **p5** Source G: James Walvin, *Leisure and Society 1890-1950* (1978), Source H: Ned Williams, *Midland Fairground Families* (1996); **p9** Source A: James Walvin, *Leisure and Society 1890-1950* (1978); **p10** Source E: Dennis Brailsford, *British Sport: a social history* (1997); **p11** Source A: H.G.Hutchinson, *The Life of Sir John Lubbock, Lord Avebury* (1914); **p12** Source D: *Encyclopaedia Britannica* (1996); **p14** Source H: Andy Mitten, *Mad for It: From Blackpool to Barcelona Football's Greatest Rivalries* (2008); **p22** Source C: Andrew Crisell, *An Introductory History of British Broadcasting* (1997); **p23** Source G: Mike Huggins, from an article *British Newsreels, Soccer and Popular Culture 1918-39* in the *International Journal of the History of Sport* (2007); **p36** Source A: Tony Mason, *Association Football and English Society 1863-1915* (1980); **p48** Source B: Colin Lewis, quoted in William Fotheringham, *Put me back on my Bike: In Search of Tom Simpson* (2002); **p53** Source A: F. Anstey, from an article *London Music Halls* in *Harper's New Monthly Magazine* (1891); **p55** Source E: Geraint Jenkins, *Wales, Yesterday and Today* (1990); **p56** Source G: David Egan, *Coal Society* (1987); **p58** Source G: T.D. Evans, Gwernogle, *Yr Ysgub Aur* (1939); **p63** Source G: Paul Terry, *Reporting in the twentieth century* (2002); **p66** Andrew Crisell, *An Introductory History of British Broadcasting* (1997); **p67** Source A: Enid Blyton, *Five on Kirrin Island* (1947); **p73** Source D: Christopher Culpin, *Making History* (1996), Source E: Alan Sillitoe, *Saturday Night and Sunday Morning* (1958); **p75** Source D: John Davies, *A History of Wales* (1990); **p81** Source B: S.Cohen, *Folk Devils and Moral Panics: the creation of mods and rockers* (1972); **p92** Source G: Gary R.Edgerton, *The Columbia History of American Television* (2007); **p132** Source F: Pat Yale, *Tourism in the UK* (2002).

Every effort has been made to trace and acknowledge ownership of copyright. The publisher will be pleased to make suitable arrangements with any copyright holders who have not been contacted.

Our thanks to the Monitoring Panel, Jean-Marc Alter, Carole Bryan-Jones, Neil Evans, Meinir Jones and Christian Rees, for their valuable guidance.

Our thanks also to Morriston Comprehensive School, Swansea, Bishop Hedley High School, Merthyr Tydfil and Hawarden High School, Deeside for taking part in the trialling process.

A Welsh medium version of this publication is also available:
Datblygiadau ym myd Chwaraeon, Hamdden a Thwristiaeth yn ystod yr 20fed Ganrif.

Contents

WHAT WERE THE MAIN CHARACTERISTICS OF SPORT IN WALES AND ENGLAND IN THE EARLY TWENTIETH CENTURY?

THE DISTINCTION BETWEEN AMATEUR AND PROFESSIONAL SPORT

The range of sports that is available to people to play and to watch today is vast. Many of these sports are relatively new but others have roots that go back a long way. Most of today's popular sports have been well supported for over a century, but the way they were organized and played was very different then.

One issue that affected all sports in the early part of the twentieth century was the distinction between **amateur** and **professional sport**. Also the level of a person's **social class** was a major factor in the type of sports that they played or watched. Some well-known sporting events such as the Henley Rowing Regatta, the Wimbledon tennis championships and the Royal Ascot horse races were typical events that marked out people's social class. The richer supporters enjoyed the luxury of the enclosures and stands while the poorer spectators were segregated in less favourable areas. These sporting events were strictly for **amateurs**. Amateurism was supposed to stand for the values that went with 'fair play' and 'sportsmanship'.

The middle and upper class men who dominated sport believed in the idea of amateurism, but they also had self-interest in blocking professionalism. This threatened to allow the working classes to compete against better-off sportsmen with success. If professional teams were to beat gentlemen amateur teams consistently, that might challenge the idea of social superiority, and that could lead to social instability. This attitude lasted for most of the twentieth century.

From an entry on amateur sports on the on-line ecyclopedia Wikipedia (2010)

In sports that were beginning to attract a mass following, such as football, cricket and boxing, **professionalism** or semi-professionalism was becoming increasingly common at the top level. Working men found it hard to play top-level sport, as they needed some payment to make up for the time missed at work. However, the organizers and administrators of amateur sports such as rugby, tennis and athletics, disliked professional performers because they thought playing for money would have a damaging effect on their sports. Professionalism meant being paid for playing, which turned a healthy sporting pastime into a job. This, it was believed, would make athletes over-competitive and prepared to win at all costs.

Despite this attitude, sport increasingly became a major part of people's lives in the first half of the twentieth century.

A photograph of the amateur Gentlemen side that played against the professional Players side in an annual cricket match at Lords (1899)

SOURCE C

The film *Chariots of Fire* [set at the 1924 Olympic Games] is organized around the contrast between the professional and the amateur. The movie tells the true story of Harold Abrahams and Eric Liddell – both gifted sprinters and both, eventually, gold medallists. Abrahams exemplifies the spirit of the professional: he is driven, highly coached, obsessed with winning and personal glory. Liddell, by contrast, embodies the spirit of the amateur: he is joyous, heartfelt, animated by the love of running and the love of God.

John S Tanner, a university vice-principal, writing in a magazine article called Amateurism and Excellence *(2003)*

TASKS

1. Explain the difference between amateur and professional in sport.

2. Use Source A and your own knowledge to explain why many people did not like professionalism in sport.

3. How useful is Source B to an historian studying sport in the early twentieth century?

4. Try to watch part of the film *Chariots of Fire*. How does the film show the way in which issues of class and social status dominated sports like athletics?

THE DEVELOPMENT AND POPULARITY OF THE MAJOR SPORTS

Rugby

The sport of rugby had spread from the English public schools and universities in the mid-nineteenth century. In Wales, the major public schools of Christ College Brecon, Llandovery College and Monmouth School all helped to promote the game.

By 1900 rugby had become very popular in South Wales. Most villages had their own teams where, unusually for the time, working men often lined up alongside people in so-called 'higher' jobs such as schoolteachers, doctors and ministers of religion.

SOURCE B

The Wales team that beat New Zealand in 1905

Successful club sides such as Cardiff, Swansea, Newport and Llanelli were well established by 1900. In 1905, Wales beat the all-conquering New Zealand All-Blacks in Cardiff and the popularity of the game soared.

However, the issue of professionalism had a major impact on rugby. In 1895, the **'broken-time'** issue had hit the game. The game's organizers, the Rugby Union, refused senior players' demands to be paid for the time they took off from their jobs to play the game. The damage this caused led to a major split and led to the setting up of the game of **rugby league** with its own rules and teams, which allowed professionalism. Rugby league became extremely popular as a working man's game in the industrial towns of the north of England. The split into rugby union and rugby league was not healed until the end of the twentieth century when rugby union eventually allowed professionalism.

Welsh rugby fans had little to enjoy between the wars. Rugby union suffered badly from the depression of the 1930s, and many talented players went to the north of England to join the professional rugby league teams. Many amateur local sides found it hard to raise sides for games. The Welsh international side was not very successful, failing to win a single **Triple Crown** between the wars. However, they did manage their first win over England and a rare 13-12 victory over the All Blacks in 1935.

TASKS

1. Explain why rugby became a popular sport in South Wales.

2. Why did rugby league begin as a sport?

3. Use Source C and your own knowledge to explain what happened to rugby in Wales in the 1930s.

4. How useful is Source A to an historian studying sport in the early twentieth century?

Football

Association football (soccer) was also widely played and supported throughout Wales and England. Football was a game largely played and supported by working people. This caused financial problems for working men who were top-class footballers. The Football Association had allowed the paying of players since 1885 and laid down a maximum wage of £4 a week in 1901. These 'salary caps' on players' wages continued to be imposed until the early 1960s when the maximum allowed had risen to £20 per week.

SOURCE D

Job	Weekly wage in 1902
Footballer	£4
Docker	£1.10
Train driver	£2.15
Bricklayer	£2.40

Figures used by Charles Korr, in his book West Ham United: the making of a football club *(1986)*

SOURCE E

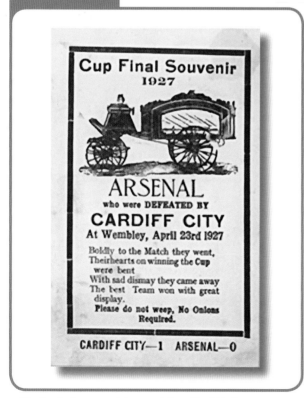

The front of a souvenir 'memorial card' sold to fans after Cardiff City's FA Cup win in 1927. On the back an inscription read 'With deepest sympathy to all English people from the Welsh'

Football became extremely popular in the whole country and Wales was no different. In the early twentieth century, the best-known side in Wales was Merthyr Town, founded in 1907, closely followed by Cardiff City in 1910. Thousands of supporters would travel by train to watch the top sides play. From the 1920s, football cemented its image as 'the people's game'. Around 6 million people paid to watch First Division football and over half a million regularly played the game in Wales and England. There were over 300 soccer clubs in South Wales alone. The 1920s were a golden age for football in Wales, culminating in Cardiff City winning the FA Cup in 1927, the only time the famous trophy has been taken out of England.

Soccer was also hit hard by the depression of the 1930s. South Wales was badly affected by unemployment and many fans could not afford to attend games. Leading clubs Aberdare Athletic and Merthyr Town, dropped out of the Football League, Swansea Town launched an appeal for money in 1935 in order to save the club from bankruptcy and Cardiff City had been relegated to the lowest division in 1931.

By 1937, the country was emerging from Depression and the crowds began to return. With increasing press and radio coverage, soccer was creating its own sporting stars. Professional players were increasingly transferred between clubs for what seemed like huge sums of money. In 1938, Arsenal's signing of ex-Merthyr player Bryn Jones from Wolves for a record £14,000 showed how much money some clubs had. (This equated to about £7 million in today's money.) This enormous fee for the time outraged politicians and led to questions about its appropriateness being asked in the House of Commons.

The connection between sport and gambling became stronger in the 1920s when the **football pools** began. Littlewoods Pools allowed people to bet each week on the results of professional football matches. Only 35 coupons were submitted in the first week in 1923, but by 1938 over ten million people were betting regularly.

TASKS

1. Why did professional football introduce a maximum wage in the early twentieth century?
2. Investigate the development of football as a popular sport in your area in the 1920s.
3. What does Source E tell you about football in the 1920s?
4. Use Source F and your own knowledge to explain what happened to many football clubs in the 1930s.
5. Explain why football became connected with gambling.

Boxing

Sports such as boxing had a long history, and were popular with both rich and poorer sections of society. Richer supporters bet huge amounts on the outcomes of fights. Many poorer people also enjoyed a flutter on bouts, and for some boxing offered a chance to earn extra cash. Travelling fairs and carnivals often had '**fighting booths**' where an ordinary man could take on a 'pro' and earn a few shillings if he won. For a few, such as Jimmy Wilde, the Tylorstown Terror, this sparked off a sensational rise to fame and fortune. Wilde had his first boxing match in a fairground in 1908. There is also evidence that women were encouraged to get into the ring and box.

Many British boxers enviously looked at the rewards for making it big in the United States where heavyweight boxers like Jack Dempsey and Joe Louis dominated the scene. Louis, 'The Brown Bomber', famously defended his title in 1937 against the former Rhondda miner, Tommy Farr, the people's champion and one of Wales' first sporting superstars. Farr earned over £10,000 for this fight. For other British boxers, the sport was not so glamorous. Audiences wanted to watch fights every week and boxers had to fight an enormous number of contests to satisfy this. Len Harvey, the British middleweight champion between the wars, fought over 400 fights. Boxers were poorly paid during the Depression in Britain, most earning between £2-£4 for a bout.

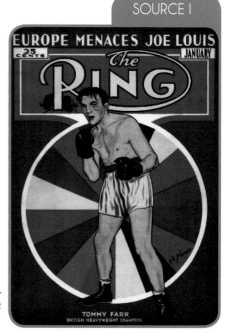

Tommy Farr, featured on the front cover of The Ring *magazine, January 1938*

TASKS

1. What were 'fighting booths'?
2. How far does Source H support the view that women rarely took part in sport at this time?
3. Find out more about the career of Tommy Farr. What did he do after retiring from boxing?

Cricket

In the early twentieth century, cricket was already regarded as the national sport of England, more so than football, which was considered a 'rougher' sport. Cricket was mainly played by better-off people, although many industrial towns and villages had flourishing teams. Paying players at the top level was common and had been for years, but cricket still kept a distinction between amateur 'gentlemen' and professional 'players'. This discrimination placed amateur and professional cricketers in separate dressing rooms and hotels, and had them enter the field by different gates and travel in different railway carriages.

Huge crowds flocked to international test matches and county games. In Wales, the popularity was so much that Glamorgan gained first-class county status in 1921. Cricket created some of Britain's sporting heroes after the First World War. Jack Hobbs and Wally Hammond were among the new breed of professional players who began to dominate cricket between the wars. Youngsters copied their heroes in the backstreets of towns and cities, using lampposts as wickets and the road as their pitch.

The famous Jack Hobbs (left) was one of the first professional cricketers to walk out through the same gate as an amateur at Lords in 1925

Children playing cricket in the street in the 1930s

International cricket reached the height of its popularity between the wars. England were world leaders and played many exciting matches against their old rivals Australia for the 'Ashes' trophy. The most famous clashes occurred when England tried to win back the Ashes in Australia in 1932. What happened put the whole issue of sportsmanship under threat. The series became known as the 'Bodyline' tour because Douglas Jardine, the England captain, ordered his fast bowlers, especially the Nottinghamshire miner, Harold Larwood, to bowl directly at the Australian batsmen's bodies. Many of the Australians were hit on the upper body and the head. For Jardine, winning was everything, and his actions and orders in the matches were highly controversial and upset relations between Australia and Britain for years.

SOURCE C

The Australian Cricket Board sent an urgent telegram to England. For the sake of cricket and sportsmanship the Australians pleaded with the English to stop hitting their batsmen. Discussions were even held in the Australian Parliament to find a way to stop the Englishmen from devastating and tarnishing the game of cricket. Eventually Jardine was ordered to refrain from his dangerous tactics. The laws of cricket were eventually changed to ensure the tactic was never repeated. The spirit of the game had to be protected at all costs.

From a website, the ABC of Cricket (2009)

Golf and tennis

Two sports that showed the class and status issue in the first half of the century were golf and lawn tennis. Better-off men ran golf. The new mobility provided by the car made it easier for people to use the growing number of private golf clubs with their restricted membership rules. However, golf was quite advanced in one way, in that it allowed amateurs and professionals to play freely alongside each other. In the 1920s there was also a surge in women playing the sport.

Lawn tennis was also largely a sport for richer people, with courts often laid out in large private gardens. The spread of middle class suburbs in the larger cities led to the establishment of successful clubs such as Garden Village in Wrexham and Dinas Powys near Cardiff. In order to encourage

SOURCE D

Public tennis and bowls facilities in Thomastown Park, Merthyr Tydfil. These were added to the park in the 1930s

more ordinary people to play the game, councils built a number of grass and hard tennis courts in public parks. Tennis received a huge boost in popularity when Fred Perry won the Wimbledon singles title in three consecutive years, 1934-1936.

TASKS

1.   In cricket, what were 'gentlemen' and 'players'?

2.   How far does Source B support the view that cricket was a game for richer people?

3.   Describe what happened in the Bodyline controversy.

4.   Use Source D and your own knowledge to explain why tennis became more popular in the 1930s.

Other sports

Another popular team game was baseball, which was especially popular among the docks communities in the port cities of Cardiff, Newport and Liverpool. International matches between Wales and England started in 1908.

SOURCE E

Courtesy of Cardiff Council Library Service

Grange Gasworks baseball team, Cardiff, 1918

SOURCE F

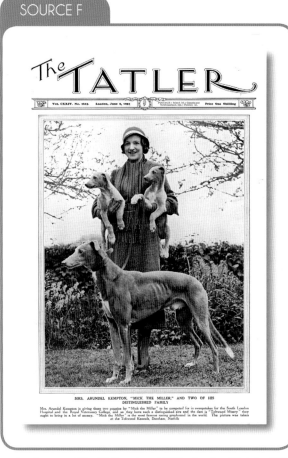

Front cover of The Tatler, *June 1932, showing Mick the Miller*

Greyhound racing grew in the 1930s. 'Going to the dogs' was an exciting night out with a chance to gamble on the races. Famous venues included the White City track in London and Manchester's Belle Vue, which introduced the electric hare. Cardiff had popular tracks at the Arms Park and Sloper Road and a track opened at Somerton Park in Newport in 1932. In 1933, over 6 million people visited dog tracks to see canine superstars such as Mick the Miller.

Cycling became very popular as recreation and as a serious competitive sport. In 1920, over 400,000 bicycles were sold; by 1935 this had increased to 4 million. Cycling clubs were common in many towns with regular 'time trials' against the clock.

Motorcycling became a major hobby. Motorbikes were much cheaper than cars and many young people owned bikes built by Triumph or Norton. Speedway – where bikes raced around an oval dirt track – began in 1928 and attracted huge crowds in the 1930s.

Aerobatic displays and air races also enthralled crowds. The public were fascinated by the exploits of female flying aces Amy Johnson and Amelia Earhart.

On a freezing cold Boxing Day 1928, the White City greyhound track on Sloper Road saw its very first speedway event on the shale oval to a crowd of 25,000. The Cardiff Dragons were the local favourites in those early years and their top riders as popular as their rugby playing counterparts. A programme from 1929 names some of the riders from the event. Crowds were entertained by the daring antics of Ronnie '*Whirlwind*' Baker, Fred '*Hurricane*' Hampson, Ray '*Sunshine*' Cannell, Jack '*Lightning*' Luke, '*Champ*' Upham, '*Genial*' Jimmy Hindle, Walter '*Nobby*' Key and Nick '*Trick*' Carter.

Mal Lee, writing in My Cardiff, *a community journalism project (2007)*

TASKS

1. Which other sports became popular during the first half of the twentieth century?
2. Find out more about the sporting achievements of Amy Johnson and Amelia Earhart.
3. How far does Source F support the view that greyhound racing was a popular pastime?
4. What does Source G tell you about speedway riders in the 1920s?

WOMEN AND SPORT

Most sports were organized and played by men. Poorer women were expected to look after the home and the family while better-off women were only expected to take part in genteel sports like lawn tennis and croquet. Even here, sport was considered to be a pastime, and it was not 'good form' for a woman to be too good at any sport. Sporting excellence was reserved for men.

Where they did occur, most women's sports were mainly individual activities. The first competitions for women in the Olympics were in sports that the organizers thought were suitable for 'ladies'.

Women were an insignificant sporting presence in the early years of the twentieth century. Even when some women made determined efforts to enjoy new forms of recreation, they met firm resistance from both men and women who believed in the philosophy that sports ought to be masculine.

James Walvin, historian, writing in a history book, Leisure and Society 1890–1950 *(1978)*

I am personally against the participation of women in sporting competition. At the Olympics the role of women should be like it was in the ancient tournaments – the crowning of victors with laurels.

Baron Pierre de Coubertin, founder of the Modern Olympics (1900)

1900	1904	1908	1912	1928
Tennis Golf	Archery	Figure skating	Swimming	Athletics

When women's events were first introduced into the Olympic Games

An advert for golf clothing for women, from the Bonwit Teller catalogue (1925)

The success of Gertrudre Ederle in swimming the channel in record time in 1926 gained much publicity and sports such as golf and tennis did a lot to encourage women to take part. These sports were mainly for better-off women, but they continued to rise in popularity. However, many middle-class women seemed to put their appearance before their performance, seeing sport more as a social rather than a physical event.

SOURCE E

When Gertrude Ederle swam the English Channel in 1926, she was not only the first woman to do so, but she knocked two hours off the best male time for the swim. It was an important moment in the history of women's sport. Six more women made the swim within months. Their success had an impact, encouraging others to take part and to develop their skills.

Dennis Brailsford, historian, writing in British Sport: a social history (1997)

Despite the attitude of the mostly male individuals in charge of sports, women began to participate in team sports. Here the class influence remained strong. 'Accepted' sports included lacrosse and hockey. However, in 1926 a group of ex-public schoolgirls from Cheltenham Ladies College played a cricket match at Malvern Boys School, going on to form a Women's Cricket Association.

Women also played football, one famous side being the Doncaster Belles who played and beat many ladies teams from other northern towns. Some games attracted over 20,000 spectators. However, this level of interest was rare. Most sport associations and the largely male spectators thought that women playing team sports was just a novelty and should be discouraged.

SOURCE F

The Dick, Kerr's Ladies football team who played at Cardiff Arms Park in 1923

SOURCE G

Complaints having been made as to football being played by women, the FA feels impelled to express its strong opinion that the game of football is quite unsuitable for females and ought not to be encouraged. The FA requests clubs belonging to the association to refuse the use of their grounds for such matches.

A resolution by the Football Association (December 1921)

As well as women playing and participating in sports more frequently, there is also evidence that an increasing number were attending events as spectators. Men remained very much in the majority but organizers were beginning to accept that there were women spectators too, and began to cater for the new audiences.

Cardiff City announced in December 1919 that they had built a ladies' 'retiring room' near the offices at Ninian Park. This was a polite way of saying that it was a women's toilet. It was also announced that the club had installed a 'convenience for gentleman' in the main stand. How everyone had managed up to then is anyone's guess!

Richard Shepherd, journalist, writing in
The Cardiff City Miscellany (2008)

TASKS

1. Explain why most women were not encouraged to take part in sport at this time.

2. Look at Sources B and E. Why do these people hold different views about the participation of women in sport?

3. How useful is Source D to an historian studying women and sport in the early twentieth century?

4. How far does Source H support the view that women did not enjoy sport at this time?

5. 'Women took part in very little sport in the first half of the twentieth century.' What evidence is there in the sources to support this statement?

THE GROWTH OF SPECTATOR SPORT

The sports mentioned above would not have developed as they did without their spectators. The first half of the twentieth century saw a massive increase in the number of spectators for the major sports. The crowds were sometimes enormous, especially from today's perspective. The record attendances of most football clubs were set during the 1920s and 1930s, or just after the Second World War. Manchester City and Chelsea set ground records of over 80,000 and there were huge crowds too at lower division grounds. Chesterfield and Halifax Town had record gates of around 30,000, as did Wrexham, whose record attendance of 29,271 was set in a local 'derby' fixture against Chester in December 1936. Why did watching live sport become so popular?

Increased leisure time

By the 1920s, most workers had become used to the idea of **paid holidays**. Since 1874 they had also got used to not working on Saturdays or at least having Saturday afternoons off. For many people this meant one thing – sport. Kick offs were standardised for 3 o'clock on a Saturday and this arrangement stayed for many decades. **Bank holidays** had been set in the 1870s and this meant that sport was also arranged for Good

Friday, Easter Monday, Christmas Day and Boxing Day when large crowds could be attracted. The Christmas Day fixtures usually kicked off at 11am to give fans the chance to also spend time at home. They lasted until the late 1950s when they were scrapped in Wales and England but continued in Scotland until 1976.

Sport played a big role in the setting of our bank holidays. In 1871, the first legislation relating to bank holidays was passed when politician Sir John Lubbock introduced the Bank Holidays Act 1871, which specified four extra days to go with Good Friday and Christmas Day. Sir John was an enthusiastic supporter of cricket and believed that workers should be encouraged to participate in and attend matches. Therefore he included in the dates of bank holidays three days when cricket games were traditionally played between villages in his home county of Kent. These were Easter Monday, Whit Monday and the last Monday in August.

H. G. Hutchinson, writing in a biography,
The Life of Sir John Lubbock (1914)

Better transport

A key factor in boosting spectator sport was the availability of transport. The railway boom of the nineteenth century meant that railways now linked up all the major cities and towns and many others in between. For organized sports such as football and cricket, this meant that vast numbers of spectators could travel easily and cheaply to support their teams. Sports grounds at this time had few controls on admissions and were mostly terraced, so huge crowds were not unusual. A crowd estimated at over 250,000 saw Bolton Wanderers win the first FA Cup Final at the newly built Wembley Stadium in 1923. The game is famously remembered as 'the White Horse final' after one policeman's attempt to control the crowd on his white police horse. Railway companies were quick to tap into the revenue to be made from spectators travelling to major sporting events, running 'special' trains just for spectators. Health and safety issues rarely existed at this time but fortunately, major disasters didn't occur until 33 fans were crushed to death at a match in Bolton in 1946.

SOURCE C

Billy the white police horse helps to clear the Wembley pitch during the 1923 FA Cup final

TASKS

1. Explain why many sports organized fixtures on Bank Holidays.
2. How did better transport lead to bigger crowds at sporting events?
3. Why is the FA cup final of 1923 a famous sporting occasion?
4. According to the author of Source D, why were football clubs 'lucky' in the period 1919-1945?
5. Find out what happened at Bolton football club in 1946. What lessons were learned?

Influence of the radio

People who didn't attend the games crowded around their radios to hear the final scores on Saturday afternoons and to check off their pools coupons. The BBC was keen to expand its audience in the 1920s and started regular **outside broadcasts** of sporting events. Events like the University Boat Race, the Derby and cricket tests were eagerly awaited by radio listeners.

The 1927 FA Cup Final between Cardiff and Arsenal was the first to be broadcast live with the *Radio Times* magazine publishing a handy numbered plan of the pitch divided into squares to help listeners work out what was happening from the radio commentary. This was the origin of the phrase '**back to square one**'. However, the radio may also have had a negative effect on sporting attendances. When the depression started to affect the crowds at football matches, the Football League banned broadcasts at its league games although the Cup Final was broadcast each year. Other sports remained popular for listeners. Millions of people tuned in to listen to Tommy Farr box Joe Louis in America for the World heavyweight title in August 1937.

Competitions and tournaments

By the 1920s, the increasing popularity of sport meant that competitions and tournaments were established to encourage rivalry and enthusiasm amongst fans. Tournaments such as the Wimbledon tennis championships and the Ashes cricket series had long been popular, as had the Football League. However, this was initially only open to a limited number of teams. As football grew in popularity, extra leagues were added – Division 2 in 1898 and Divisions 3 north and south in 1921. These leagues, with their points system and promotion and relegation for teams, ensured support all season long.

The knockout FA cup competition was also a huge draw. By 1946, fifty-eight of the eighty-four football ground records listed had been set at F.A. Cup matches, where the 'sudden-death' knock-out format held special appeal. Other popular matches were local 'derbies', holiday games, and battles involving promotion and relegation. Rugby union had its Home International tournament, which became the Five Nations when France joined in 1910. Rugby union did not have a league for its club teams though, thinking this might lead to too much competition. Rugby league had no such worries – their league was established in 1922 and rivalled soccer for crowds in the northern towns of England.

Town rivalries

Another factor that led to many sports becoming great entertainment was the rivalry that was created. Sporting rivalry between villages and towns was nothing new. Henry VIII had even banned a Tudor version of football because of the bad feeling it generated. In the early twentieth century, local **derby matches** in football and rugby, the 'Roses' cricket fixtures between Lancashire and Yorkshire and rugby internationals between Wales and England became great occasions to be relished and looked forward to for months. These usually took place without the violence and hooliganism that was to blight spectator sport in the later years of the twentieth century.

The rivalry between Liverpool and Manchester United football clubs can be considered as a reflection of one which already had existed between the two cities since industrial times. During this time both cities were competing with each other for supremacy in the north-west, with Manchester famous for its manufacturing prowess while Liverpool was famous for the importance of its port. Once the Manchester Ship Canal was built, ships could bypass Liverpool and transport goods directly into Manchester. This caused job losses at the port and resentment from the local people of Liverpool. This spilled over into many areas, including sport. To rub it in, the crest of Manchester United displayed a ship representing the importance of the canal.

From a website highlighting the major football derbies (2008)

The 1901 Good Friday encounter between Newcastle and Sunderland at St James' Park had to be abandoned as up to 70,000 fans made their way into a ground which had a capacity of 30,000. The news was met with anger, and rioting followed, with a number of fans injured. However, in general, although the derby attracted huge crowds, there is little evidence to suggest any animosity between the two sets of supporters in the inter-war period.

Andy Mitten, sports historian, writing in Mad For It: Football's greatest rivalries *(2008)*

TASKS

1. Make a list of the main factors that caused spectator sport to grow in the first half of the twentieth century.

2. What sports were popular on the radio in the 1920s and 1930s?

3. What is the origin of the phrase 'back to square one'?

4. How did the radio have a negative effect on sporting crowds?

5. Why were the development of leagues and cups important in attracting crowds?

6. How useful is Source F to an historian studying the popularity of sport in this period?

7. Choose a local derby match from your area. Explain why this game attracts so much local attention.

This section provides guidance on how to answer question 1(a) from Units 1 and 2. It is a source comprehension question, which is worth 2 marks.

Question 1(a) – comprehension of a visual source

What does Source A show you about sporting events during this period? [2 marks]

SOURCE A

Fans at the 1923 FA Cup final at Wembley Stadium

Tips on how to answer

This is an inference question involving the comprehension of a visual source.

- You are being asked to **look into the picture** and **pick out** relevant details.
- You must also **make use of the statement written below the source**, which is intended to provide you with additional information.
- You must **only comment on what you can see** in the picture and what is written immediately below the source. **Do not** bring in additional factual knowledge, as this will not score you marks.
- To obtain maximum marks you will need to **pick out at least two relevant points** that are well developed and supported.

Candidate response

Source A shows a crowd of supporters on the pitch at the FA Cup Final in 1923. The stands in the ground are packed and it is likely that these fans were on the pitch because of overcrowding. The picture shows that most supporters at football matches were men and that police were used to control the crowds. Obviously games like these were very popular.

The candidate has made a number of valid observations based on the source and the caption. There is a clear understanding that crowds were huge for some events and it is inferred that the majority of supporters were men. This is an answer worthy of 2 marks.

Now you have a go

SOURCE B

Fans on their way to a football match in the 1920s

Question

What does Source B show you about spectator sport during the 1920s?

CHAPTER 2

HOW IMPORTANT HAS THE CONTRIBUTION OF SPORTING HEROES BEEN FOR THE DEVELOPMENT OF SPORT IN WALES AND ENGLAND IN THE TWENTIETH CENTURY?

THE INFUENCE OF THE MEDIA UP TO THE 1970s

Images and reports of sport have been found in all the media used in the twentieth century. In the period up to the 1970s, the presentation of these images and reports could be found mostly in the printed word in newspapers, magazines, comics and books. Other important ways of getting information about sport were the radio, cinema and television, although the latter was much more influential after the 1970s.

The media had a huge influence on the development of sport up to the 1970s; they encouraged a following for certain sports, especially among those people who could not get to sporting events. They also helped to create the idea of the sporting heroes and idols that dominated headlines in much the same way as they do today.

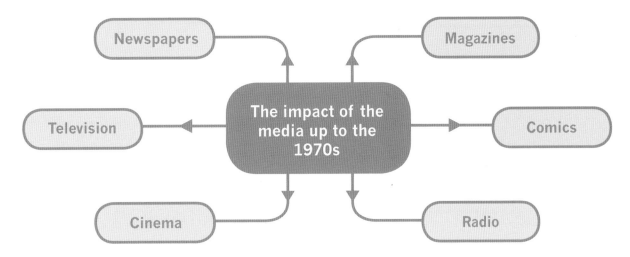

Each format had its own targeted audience and presented sport in its own special way, telling the stories and presenting the facts in a manner that ensured its audience came back for more. Sport needed media coverage for the interest and possible finance it brought and the media needed sport to attract readers and listeners.

The written media – newspapers, magazines and comics

Newspapers

People have had access to written words about sport for a long time. Because of its popularity, sport has been used to sell newspapers and editors have used sensational headlines about sporting personalities and events in order to encourage people to buy newspapers. Most newspapers always had separate sports pages and reporters and photographers were employed specifically to collect news and pictures about sport. They also covered the popular, high profile sports such as football, rugby, horse racing and cricket. Millions of people bought newspapers every day in the twentieth century and the newspapers considerably influenced the popularity of individuals, teams and sporting events.

SOURCE A

A newspaper headline about the exploits of the famous Australian cricketer Donald Bradman (July 1934)

Journalists and reporters

Cricket, possibly because of its elite status in society, regularly attracted famous writers as journalists. The *Manchester Guardian* in the first half of the 20th century employed Neville Cardus as its cricket reporter. Cardus was later knighted for his services to journalism. The first London Olympic Games in 1908 attracted such widespread public interest that many newspapers assigned their very best known writers to the event. The *Daily Mail* even had Sir Arthur Conan Doyle, the author of the Sherlock Holmes stories, to report on the finish of the first ever 26-mile, 385-yard marathon.

SOURCE B

Arthur Conan Doyle reported on the dramatic finish of the first ever Olympic marathon in London in 1908. This photograph shows Dorando Pietri being helped over the finishing line; he was later disqualified

Some newspapers began to adopt a policy of hiring former sports stars to write columns, which were often ghost written. These included *The Sunday Times*, with 1924 Olympic 100 m champion Harold Abrahams, or the *London Evening News*, which used former England cricket captain Sir Leonard Hutton in the 1950s. These ensured that many people bought the newspaper just to read the words of their heroes.

There were even newspapers dedicated to sport, which took an active role in generating popularity. The annual Polytechnic Marathon in London, staged over the 1908 Olympic route was sponsored by *Sporting Life*, which was a daily newspaper that sought to cover all sporting events. In France, the sports newspaper *L'Auto* played an influential part in the history of sport when it announced in 1903 that it would stage an annual bicycle race around the country. The *Tour de France* was born, and the newspaper's role in its foundation is still reflected today in the leading rider wearing a yellow jersey – the colour of the paper on which *L'Auto* was published. Promotion of sport in these newspapers led to great interest in the sports and the participants.

After the Second World War, the sports sections of British national daily and Sunday newspapers continued to expand. Many regional newspapers would produce **special results editions** rushed out on Saturday evenings, such as the famous 'pink 'un' published by the *South Wales Echo*.

A cycling race in the 1920s

The pink *Football Echo* used to have two editions in its heyday. They had one that was on the streets twenty minutes after the final whistle. They would have half-time match reports in there and all the final scores on the last page. About quarter to seven they would bring out a full edition with full reports, up-to-date league tables and people would queue for them. They would sell about 80,000 copies every Saturday.

Ken Gorman, who worked as a reporter on the Football Echo *in the 1960s (2006)*

Photography

The 1950s and 1960s saw a rapid growth in sports coverage with the development of specialist sports news and photographic agencies. Photographer Tony Duffy founded the picture agency *All Sport* in south London in 1964. He produced iconic photography such as the image of the American long jumper Bob Beamon flying through the air towards his world record at the 1968 Mexico City Olympics. The clever **marketing** of its images saw sports photography grow into a worldwide business.

The iconic photograph of Bob Beamon breaking the world long jump record at the Mexico Olympics in 1968

1. Explain why many newspapers publish features about sport.

2. Why did newspapers start to use sports stars to write some of their articles?

3. Give some ways in which newspapers were directly involved in influencing sport in the early twentieth century.

4. How useful is Source D to an historian studying the influence of newspapers on sport in the mid twentieth century?

5. Use Source E and your own knowledge to explain how sports photography helped to create sports stars and heroes.

Magazines

As well as newspapers, the first half of the twentieth century saw the publication of many magazines devoted to the major sports. One of the most well known was *The Cricketer*, a magazine founded in 1921 by Sir Pelham Warner, the ex-England captain turned cricket writer. There were also many magazines devoted to football. The *Topical Times* was the first weekly magazine that had a high level of football related content. It also featured boxing, horseracing and an action short story. It was published from 1919-1940. The magazine also produced the glossy *Topical Times* cards that showcased leading footballers, as a free gift with each edition. These were eagerly collected and swapped by young readers.

The *Football Pictorial and Illustrated Review* was the first football magazine for adults. It went on sale in 1935. In the first edition it stated:

SOURCE A

THOMAS G. JONES, Everton F.C. TOPICAL TIMES.

A Topical Times *card showing footballer Thomas G Jones of Everton and Wales (1939)*

SOURCE B

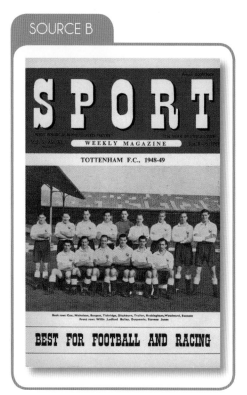

The cover of Sport Weekly Magazine, January 1949

"The directors feel happy in the knowledge to be the first publishers in London to issue such a specialised football journal". Another similar publication was *Sport Weekly Magazine*, first seen in 1938 and featuring football, horse racing, rugby and boxing.

By the 1950s, specialist sports magazines had begun to develop, covering sports ranging from athletics to yachting. They aimed to inform the reader on how to develop their own skills and ability, provide information about particular personalities and forthcoming events as well as advertising products that were related to sport.

The success of England in the football World Cup in 1966 and Scottish and English clubs in European competition in 1967-68 saw a surge in the popularity of soccer magazines, especially for younger readers. One of these was *Shoot*, which was launched in 1969 and sold over 100,000 copies a week at its height.

Comics

Another type of written medium that was highly influential in creating interest in sport was the comic, especially for boys and young men. Comics featured **fictional sports stars** that became almost as famous as the real ones. One of the most popular featured a character called Alf Tupper. He was a working class, hard as nails runner, whose adventures appeared first in the *Rover* in 1949 and continued for almost 40 years, under the title *The Tough of the Track*.

The *Roy of the Rovers* cartoon strip began in 1954 as a weekly feature in the comic *Tiger*. After twenty years of continued popularity, the strip was successful enough to have its own weekly comic, which was launched in 1976. There were also hardback annuals and holiday specials featuring Roy and his superstar lifestyle.

Billy's Boots was another popular British comic strip with a sporting hero. Billy had found an old pair of boots in his grandmother's house that turned him into a heroic footballer. The comic appeared for the first time in the first issue of *Scorcher* in 1970, and later moved to *Tiger* when the two comics merged in 1974. Comic strips rarely featured girls in sport although comics like *Bunty* and *Judy* did have stories in which girls played team sports like hockey or lacrosse.

TASKS

1. How did sports magazines differ from newspapers?
2. How did sports magazines try to attract readers?
3. Why did many comics feature sporting stories?
4. Find out more about either Alf Tupper, Roy of the Rovers or Billy's Boots. Why do you think these fictional characters were so popular?
5. Why do you think that few comic strips featured stories about female sports characters?
6. How useful is Source C to an historian studying the link between comics and sport?

The non-written media
– radio, the cinema and television

Radio

The influence of radio in developing the popularity of sport and sporting heroes was considerable in the 1930s and it remained strong in the period after 1945. As well as continuing to broadcast live events, results programmes and features became standard. In 1948, the BBC broadcast the first ever edition of *Sports Report* at 5.00 pm on a Saturday afternoon. The day's football results were read out immediately after the signature tune, followed by brief reports on the day's leading games. Other sports would also feature, especially horse racing. This was the forerunner to modern day radio and television results shows and often made celebrities of the commentators and announcers as well.

Television

The first live televised football match in Britain was actually in 1937, but television coverage of sport really took off in the 1960s. Both BBC and ITV introduced Saturday afternoon sports shows, which became hugely popular in the 1960s and 1970s. The BBC launched *Grandstand* in 1958, which covered nearly every major sporting event in Britain, such as the FA Cup final, Wimbledon, the Grand National and Test match cricket, as well as major international events like the Olympic Games and the football World Cup. The programme lasted until 2007 when it became a casualty of the growth of satellite television. Like radio, shows like *Grandstand* highlighted all the top sporting stars and also made household names of the **commentators** like Bill MacLaren, Eddie Waring, David Coleman and Murray Walker.

Not to be outdone, by the mid-1960s ITV had launched its own Saturday sports programme, *World of Sport*. The show included popular features such as *On the Ball* (a preview of the day's football action), the *ITV Seven* (horse racing), and wrestling. **Minority sports** were a feature throughout its run. It showed sports not seen elsewhere, such as women's hockey, netball, lacrosse, water skiing and Gaelic football.

Both channels were able to show the 1966 World Cup final, which England won by beating West Germany 4-2. Many households rented televisions for the first time just for the tournament and the influence of television on sport now became huge. The final remains the most watched event ever on British television, attracting 32.6 million viewers. Both channels also saw the value of screening domestic football. The BBC had started *Match of the Day* in 1964 and ITV began *The Big Match* in 1968. These also attracted big viewing audiences and players became recognizable stars.

I couldn't wait for *Sports Report* each Saturday. In those days of little or no up-to-the minute news, this would be the first we knew of the final score for our favourite team. In our house the ritual was always the same – my dad, pencil at the ready, the Daily Express folded at the fixtures column, carefully writing down the scores as John Webster read them out. The tone of his voice at the beginning of each game gave a clue to the final score – home win, away win or draw!

David Watkins, discussing his love of radio in the 1950s, in an interview published in a local newspaper (2008)

World of Sport always found it hard to compete with *Grandstand*. The BBC had purchased the rights to as many established sporting events as it could. A joke of the period was that the BBC were going through the list of sports in alphabetical order and had run out of cash before it reached wrestling, which is how ITV got it.

From an article in the Daily Mail *newspaper, commenting on the BBC decision to scrap Grandstand in 2007*

Prior to 1966, live television coverage of the World Cup in Britain was patchy. When the tournament took place in Chile in 1962, film of matches had to be rushed by motorcycle courier to the airport, where it was sent to the USA to be edited and transmitted back to London, and a nightly programme was put out by the BBC, usually around three days after the match had been played. Within four years, however, developments in satellite technology meant that matches could be shown live across the world.

Andrew Crisell, historian, writing in An Introductory History of British Broadcasting *(2002)*

I remember the final well. My dad had got a TV from Rediffusion just for the World Cup. During the match, I could not stand the strain any longer so I went out for a walk. The streets were deserted. No cars on the road or people in the street. I walked past a neighbour's house as England scored the final goal to clinch the cup and was greeted by the householder, who came running out shouting, "We won! We won!" I rushed home and my dad was holding my baby sister up to the TV and said, "My darling, you will never see this again in your lifetime". Naturally, she is still waiting for him to be proven wrong.

Ann Hungerford, who was 7 years old in 1966, remembering the World Cup Final of that year. She was interviewed for a primary school project on the World Cup in 2010

George Best, playing for Manchester United in 1968 in a game shown later on Match of the Day

Cinema

The other medium that helped to popularise sport and sporting stars was the cinema. During the 1930s, the cinema was the only place where fans could see their heroes. Every cinema showed regular **newsreels** in between the films, which showed items of topical interest. The newsreel was the main source of news and sport for millions of cinema goers until television took on the role in the 1960s.

Between the wars soccer was the leading national sport in Britain. But far more people watched the brief clips of soccer on the newsreels in the cinema than ever watched football on the pitch. Newsreels were a crucial factor in the development of football as a mass sport, making stars of hundreds of players.

Mike Huggins, an historian writing in British newsreels, soccer and popular culture 1918–39 *(2007)*

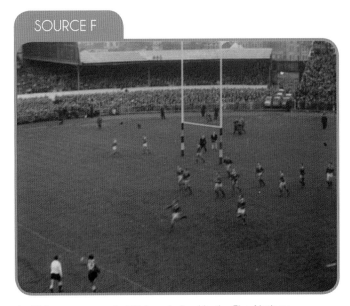

A still from a newsreel of Wales v Ireland in the Five Nations rugby championship in 1965

The popularity of sport and the coverage and publicity provided by the range of media meant that many sportsmen and sportswomen became very well known. This trend became increasingly common in the 1930s and continued after the Second World War. As the twentieth century progressed, more and more athletes became **household names** for their exploits. The sporting idol or celebrity was here to stay.

SPORTING STARS

The idea of the sporting star who becomes a household name and whose exploits are avidly followed by huge numbers of fans did not start in the later twentieth century. Each era throws up its own stars. Some of these are still remembered by many people, others are less well known, but in their own way each played a crucial role in the development of their sport. They have all had a great impact in some way – local, national or international.

It is impossible to identify a definitive list of sporting stars. Ask people of any age and, assuming they are interested in sport, they will come up with a different list.

The chart opposite shows this. A selection of people of different ages were asked to nominate their sporting idols or heroes and to briefly explain their choices. The results were very different but even the ones who professed to have little or no interest in sport were able to give a choice.

Dewi Davies, a man in his 80s, chose:

Gareth Edwards – he stood for all that was good in Welsh rugby in the 1970s

Howard Winstone – a world boxing champion from Merthyr Tydfil

Stanley Matthews – the 'magician' – the best footballer I have ever seen

Mair Jones, a woman in her 70s, chose:

John Charles – the 'Gentle Giant', a nickname well deserved

Virginia Wade – the last British woman to win Wimbledon

Fanny Blankers-Koen – the star of the 1948 Olympics in London

Doug Olsen, a man in his 60s, chose:

Mohammed Ali – voted the sporting icon of the twentieth century – who am I to disagree?

George Best – the best footballer of all time – bar none

Brian Clark – scored the goal for Cardiff that beat Real Madrid in 1971

Ann Howard, a woman in her 50s, chose:

Bob Stokoe – manager of Sunderland when they won the FA Cup in 1973

Evonne Goolagong – an Australian aboriginal player who won Wimbledon twice

Steve Redgrave – proved that diabetics can succeed at the highest level in sport

Richard Davies, a man in his 40s, chose:

Eric Liddell – the man who wouldn't run on a Sunday – I remember studying it in RE and seeing it in Chariots of Fire

Lasse Viren – the only dog to win two Olympic gold medals – only joking!

Steve Ovett – I always preferred him to Seb Coe, more of a rebel

Claire Thomas, a woman in her 30s, chose:

Daley Thompson – he made me laugh when I was a little girl

Tanni Grey-Thompson – because of what she has done for disabled athletes

Caster Semenya – who has shown great dignity despite all her critics who are just jealous of her talent

Brian Allen, a man in his 20s, chose:

Nasser Hussein – the first cricketer of Asian origin to captain England

Joe Calzaghe – a great boxer who eventually got the acclaim he deserved

Roger Federer – is he the best tennis player of all time? Probably

Emma Foster, a teenager, chose:

Shane Williams – because he is cute

Stephen Jones – he scores all the points for Wales

Jonathan Foster – because he is my brother and he always plays well

THE IMPACT OF SPORTING STARS

It is impossible to single out individuals really, but these have all been highly praised in their own times for their contribution to and impact on the development of sport and wider society.

Fred Perry

The greatest player produced by the UK in the twentieth century, Fred Perry won Wimbledon in three consecutive years, captured a trio of U.S. Championships, and joined an elite cast of male players in recording victories at all four major championships. Energetic, imposing, charismatic, full of self-conviction, Perry carried himself with immense poise and professionalism.

From the citation to include Fred Perry in the International Tennis Hall of Fame (1995)

Fred Perry, who won Wimbledon in 1936

Len Hutton

Widely regarded as the finest England batsman after the Second World War, Len Hutton broke the world-record score in his sixth Test. He was also England's first professional captain. He was knighted for his contribution to cricket in 1956

From the obituary for Len Hutton published in *Wisden* (1990)

Len Hutton batting for England in 1954

Gareth Edwards

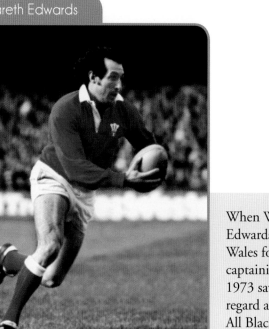

When Wales enjoyed its finest decade of rugby success, Gareth Edwards was an ever-present factor. At 19, Gareth represented Wales for the first time against France. The following season he was captaining the side, the youngest player ever to do so.
1973 saw the Gareth Edwards try that connoisseurs of the game still regard as the finest ever scored. It was for the Barbarians against the All Blacks. In the era in which rugby defined Wales to the world, Edwards defined rugby to Wales.

Gareth Edwards playing for Wales against Argentina in 1976

From the website, *100 Welsh heroes* (2003)

Famous, handsome and very, very rich, David Beckham has become a global celebrity and a national icon. His career reflects the transformation of football from beautiful game to global product. Yet the more soulless his sport becomes, the more down-to-earth Beckham himself seems to be. What marks him out is his basic decency and lack of self-importance unknown in celebrity-land. He fronts the English campaign to host the 2018 World Cup and he goes to Afghanistan to salute the troops.

From an editorial in *The Guardian* newspaper (August 2010)

David Beckham playing for England in 2009

Mary Rand

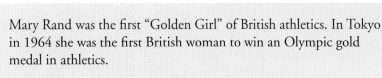

Mary Rand was the first "Golden Girl" of British athletics. In Tokyo in 1964 she was the first British woman to win an Olympic gold medal in athletics.

Dear Mary,
They have marked out your jump in the Market Square in town. It's all drawn out on the pavement, outside the shops so that people can always see it. It's beautiful how they've done it. I stopped the other day and listened to some American tourists as they stopped to examine it. The man said 'Jesus, honey, can you believe how far this girl jumped?'

From a letter written to Mary by her mother in 1968. Mary had emigrated to America.

Mary Rand winning a gold medal at the 1966 Commonwealth Games

Tanni Grey-Thompson

Baroness Tanni Grey-Thompson, Britain's most famous paralympian athlete visited Beirut on April 12, 2010 as part of a regional tour. The aim of her visit was to discuss with the Lebanese Olympic and Paralympics committees their preparations for the London 2012 Olympics. Tanni also addressed an audience of individuals with special needs, disabled athletes and other leading sports and political figures. She spoke about human rights and the values of social inclusiveness for disabled people.

Press release from the British Embassy in the Lebanon (August 2010)

Tanni Grey-Thompson competing at the Paralympic Games in Sydney in 2000

Kelly Holmes is the first British woman to win two Olympic gold medals, and the country's first double gold medallist at the same games since Albert Hill in 1920. Her time of 3 minutes 57.90 seconds in the 1500 m final also set a new British record for the distance. For her achievements she won numerous awards and was appointed a dame by the Queen in 2005. She retired from athletics in 2005 and has since made a number of television appearances and is the President of Commonwealth Games England.

From the website *Black Presence in Britain* (2010)

Kelly Holmes winning the 1500 m Gold Medal at the 2002 Commonwealth Games

Nicole Cooke winning the World Cycling Championship in 2008

What an achievement, winning Olympic Gold on top of all her other successes. I used to cycle with Cardiff Ajax Club, and remember seeing Nicole start her cycling career at Maindy cycle track when she was very young. She is a credit to Wales and to our sport. She will get my vote for sports personality of the year, and I hope she wins it as well instead of some poncy footballer. Well done Nicole.

Jesse Davies, posting on the BBC Wales South East message board (2008)

TASKS

1. Describe the achievements of one male and one female sports star of your choice.

2. Create a website that features the achievements of one sports star of your choice. This star must be from pre1980.

3. Interview people of different ages about their sports idols. Make up a display based on the findings. This can be grouped by age, sex or sport.

4. Working in groups, find out more about the impact that sports stars can have. Then use your research to answer the question: *How important has the contribution of sporting heroes been for the development of sport in Wales and England?*

Examination practice

This section provides guidance on how to answer question 1(b) from Units 1 and 2. It is a source comprehension question, which is linked to the recall of your own knowledge and it is worth 4 marks.

Question 1(b) – comprehension of a source and the recall of own knowledge

Use the information in Source A and your own knowledge to explain how the media popularised sport in the mid twentieth century. [4 marks]

SOURCE A

The media really began to recognise the popularity of sport in the mid-twentieth century. Newspapers began to dedicate many pages to sport and some even had separate sports sections. Magazines were started to cater for the interests of the growing army of sports fans.

Taken from a website

Tips on how to answer

- Read through the source, **underlining or highlighting** the key points.
- In your answer you should **try to rephrase and explain these points** in your own words.
- Aim to bring in your own **background knowledge** to expand upon these points.
- Think about any **other relevant factors** that are not included in the source and bring them into your answer.
- To obtain maximum marks **you need to do two things**: refer to information from the source and add to this information from your own knowledge of this topic area.

Response by candidate one

The media are things like papers and the TV. These always have lots of sport in them because people are interested in sport. Sport is on the back pages of the papers and it is always on the TV. People like sport because it is fun and they can shout for their own team. It was the papers and the TV that made sport popular.

> General material that does not answer the question set

> The last sentence gets some credit

Examiner's comment

This answer lacks any real development. The candidate has demonstrated little attempt to explain how the media popularised sport. There is no attempt to place the source into its historical context and the weak references to television are not really accurate in the context of the question. They may be awarded one mark for the final sentence.

Response by candidate two

The media was really important in popularising sport in the mid twentieth century. As Source A shows, a major role was played by the newspapers which covered huge sporting events like the Olympics and the FA Cup.
In Cardiff, there were sports papers like the *Football Echo* that came out on Saturdays. Magazines like the *Topical Times* began to come out for really dedicated fans and they gave away collectors cards. Even comics got in on the act with popular sports cartoons in the 1950s. However, I think that the most important way of popularising sport was the radio and the cinema newsreel because the fans could see and hear the events then.

Specific reference to the source

Use of own knowledge to expand upon information provided in the source

Gives further examples of media coverage

Starts to drift here into a judgement, which is not needed

Examiner's comment

This is a well-developed answer. The candidate demonstrates a sound understanding of this topic and has worked the source material well. There is a good blend of own knowledge to explain and expand upon the information given in the source. There is some context relating to the mid-twentieth century. The answer does drift at the end where the candidate appears to be making a judgement on the importance of different types of media, but the answer has already done enough for the four marks.

Now you have a go

SOURCE B

Television had little real influence on popularising sport until the 1960s. However, the amount of sport shown on BBC and ITV grew, with shows like *Grandstand* and *Match of the Day* becoming very popular with audiences and making stars of the players and commentators.

From a school textbook

Question

Use the information in Source B and your own knowledge to explain why television was able to popularise sport in the 1960s.

[4 marks]

CHAPTER 3

HOW HAS SPORT IN WALES AND ENGLAND BEEN AFFECTED BY CHANGES IN SOCIETY IN THE LATE TWENTIETH CENTURY?

OPPORTUNITIES FOR PARTICIPATION AND RECREATION IN THE LATE TWENTIETH CENTURY

Increased leisure time

There was a huge growth in participation in sports and recreation in Britain in the later twentieth century, especially from the 1960s. This was due to a number of general factors such as:

- Increased **leisure time**;

- Fuller employment and more disposable income;

- Better transport and wider car ownership;

- Greater media coverage of sports and recreation;

- Growing concerns about health and fitness.

Also there were a number of more specific factors, which led to more opportunities to take part in sport and recreation, both as a participant and as a spectator.

Improved facilities

As the country returned to some sort of normality after the Second World War, successive governments responded to a growing demand for new sporting facilities by encouraging the building of both private and publicly owned **indoor sports centres**.

© Crown copyright: RCAHMW

The Wales Empire Pool in Cardiff, built for the Empire Games in 1958

The Wales Empire swimming pool was built for the 1958 Empire Games, which were held in Cardiff. The first purpose-built sports centre in England was built at Harlow in Essex in 1964. The Wales Institute of Sport in Cardiff was built in 1971.

SOURCE B

In 1964, there was only one sports hall in Great Britain, in Harlow. Now the local sports centre has become as much a part of the fabric of community life as the local bank, school or doctor's surgery.

From a report on sports facilities in Essex, 2007–2020 written by Strategic Leisure Limited (2006)

Indoor sports centres encouraged many people to participate in 'new' sports, particularly team sports like basketball and volleyball, which began to be more common in schools in Wales and England. Badminton and squash increased in popularity, as did gymnastics, especially after Olga Korbut, a young Russian gymnast, captured people's hearts at the 1972 Olympic Games in Munich.

SOURCE C

Olga Korbut is an amazing athlete with four Olympic gold medals to her credit, but it is not this feat for which she is most remembered. The media whirl which surrounded her 1972 Olympic debut caused a surge of young girls to join their local gymnastic clubs, and a sport which had seldom been noticed previously now made headlines.

From an article on the legacy of Olga Korbut on Wikipedia (2005)

There were only a handful of gymnastics clubs in South Wales in the 1960s: by 2000 there were over 60 flourishing clubs in the region. The amount of sporting activity taken by people began to rise quite clearly as more opportunities were provided.

SOURCE D

When the club got floodlights in the mid 1970s, it was great. We played on a Saturday and also now every Tuesday. Clubs without lights wanted to play us and crowds flocked in to see the local derbies against rivals like Glynneath, Mountain Ash and Rhymney. In the 1979–80 season I played over 50 games for the firsts. The pitch was in a mess at the end of the season though!

Steve Howard, a player for Merthyr RFC in the 1970s and 1980s remembering the effect of floodlights in a local history publication (2000)

In the 1960s, football and rugby grounds like Rodney Parade in Newport began to introduce floodlights. These were initially meant for evening training, but they allowed clubs to offer mid-week fixtures that brought in large crowds and increased income.

The development of synthetic outdoor playing surfaces in the 1970s and 1980s also allowed more opportunities for training and playing. Sports like hockey, football, athletics and tennis benefited most from this development.

SOURCE E

Artificial pitches have transformed the game of hockey, as it allows players to control the ball more easily and make the game much faster. Synthetic turf provides the right balance of ball bounce, resistance, friction and shock absorption. This makes it a perfect pitch to play on all year round, in all weather conditions.

From an advertising brochure by a company that manufactures synthetic pitches, Perfectly Green (2006)

Facility	1972	1997
Sports Halls	11	180
Swimming Pools	25	143
Golf Courses	104	176
Squash Courts	86	442
Synthetic athletic tracks	0	14
Indoor tennis centres	0	9
Artificial pitches	0	72
Indoor bowls halls	0	27
Ice rinks	0	2

Figures showing increasing sports facilities in Wales 1972–1997, published by the Sports Council for Wales (1999)

TASKS

1. Explain why there was an increase in participation in sport and recreation in the late twentieth century.

2. Describe the improvements in sports facilities that took place after the Second World War.

3. Why was Olga Korbut an influential figure in sport in the 1970s?

4. Use Source F as a template to investigate the availability of sports facilities in your area.

5. Use Source D and your own knowledge to explain why the introduction of floodlights was important for many sports clubs.

The push for health and fitness – the obesity 'epidemic'

People became more interested in health and fitness as the twentieth century progressed. In the 1970s, many people took up jogging, whilst in the 1980s aerobics classes became very popular, especially with women.

Despite the rise in activity, by the end of the twentieth century, there was increasing medical and government concern over issues like **obesity** and lack of exercise. This led to a rise in the number of **private gyms** and sports complexes; this, in turn, has seen more people take advantage of these facilities, which they can fit into their daily work routine.

SOURCE A

In 1984, I was captain of Wellingborough RFC. One of the players complained that training was boring and we should try something different. So I got my sister to hold an aerobics session for the players. The moaner was shattered. He couldn't play on Saturday because he was still aching from the aerobics. He didn't moan about training any more.

Billy Gall, former Wellingborough RFC player, remembering an incident in the 1984–85 season

Exercise machines available in a modern gym

New complexes were built and older sports centres upgraded to cater for a demand for more sophisticated fitness facilities. They offered swimming pools, individual programmes and hi-tech equipment like running machines.

Walking and cycling had been popular leisure activities throughout the twentieth century. These activities were now publicised as excellent ways to keep healthy while also enjoying the open air.

There has been a surge in the popularity of outdoor activities including climbing, skiing, canoeing and mountain biking. Ironically, it was the growth in private car ownership that enabled more people to reach remoter parts of the countryside. At the same time, young people were offered more chances to take part in outdoor activities through schools and youth clubs.

Many local authorities built 'activity centres' for the public. Plas Menai in North Wales, built by the Sports Council for Wales in 1986, became one of Britain's leading national sports centres, offering a range of activities from white water rafting, canoeing and sailing to caving, rock climbing and mountain biking.

SOURCE C

Sport / activity	1994	2004
Walking	22	38
Swimming	14	9
Cycling	6	12
Golf	4	7
Football	6	10
Aerobics / gym	3	14

Figures showing the percentage of people participating in sport in Wales between 1994–2004, published by the Sports Council for Wales (2005)

SOURCE D

Green fitness has become increasingly important. Getting fit in the great outdoors has always been popular, but now it is a great way of making sure that your workout doesn't leave a huge carbon footprint. Research shows that over 20% of people are turning to cheaper ways to exercise during the recession and are going walking and cycling at the weekends – just like they did during the 1930s!

Joanne Knight, editor of Women's Fitness, *writing in an article in the magazine (2009)*

1. Explain why there was a growth in private sports facilities in recent years.

2. How useful is Source C to an historian studying sporting activities in the last 20 years?

3. Describe the growth in popularity of outdoor sports in the late twentieth century.

4. Using Source C as a template, carry out a survey of sporting activities carried out by people in your school.

5. How far does Source D support the view that outdoor sports are becoming more popular?

6. Discuss the view that the biggest change in sports facilities in the last 30 years has been the building of local leisure centres.

Disabled sports

Organized sport for persons with physical disabilities only really developed after the Second World War. In response to the needs of large numbers of injured ex-service members and civilians, sport was introduced as a key part of rehabilitation. Sport for rehabilitation then grew into recreational sport and then into competitive sport. In 1948, while the Olympic Games were being held in London, a sports competition for wheelchair athletes was held at Stoke Mandeville Hospital. This was the origin of the Stoke Mandeville Games, which evolved into the modern **Paralympic Games** that has led to disabled athletes such as Tanni Grey Thompson and Ellie Simmonds becoming very well known.

SOURCE A

Leading disabled athlete Oscar Pistorius, known as the 'Blade Runner'

SOURCE B

Disability Sport Wales aims to:

*   increase the number of disabled people who actively participate in sports clubs, groups and sessions;
*   create new and further develop existing opportunities for disabled people to compete in sport at local, regional and national level.

Part of the mission statement for the organization Disability Sport Wales (2006)

Sport for persons with intellectual disabilities began to be organized in the 1960s through the Special Olympics movement. In 1968 the first international Special Olympics were held in Chicago. Today, the Special Olympics provides training and competition in a variety of sports for persons with intellectual disabilities.

Many organizations have been established to provide facilities for disabled people to participate in sporting activities. These organizations work closely with local authorities to encourage participation. Unfortunately it seems that progress has been slow with disabled people citing several barriers against participation. These include transport, lack of money, lack of suitable clubs and a lack of information.

Regular participation in sport by disabled people is lower across all age groups than participation by non-disabled people. This applies to both males and females. In 2006 8.8% of disabled people took part in sport and active recreation three times a week. The percentage of non-disabled people was 17%. In 2007, the ratio was 9.1% to 18% and in 2008 it was 8.7% to 19%.

From a report by the English Federation of Disability sports (2009)

TASKS

1. Describe the growth of sport for disabled people since 1945.

2. Outline some the problems faced by disabled people in participating in sport.

3. How useful is Source C in finding out about participation in sport by disabled people?

Women and sport

In the later twentieth century women have had far more opportunity to participate in sport than ever before. Women's participation in sport grew considerably over the second half of the twentieth century. Women had played a major role in many sports in the earlier decades, but the media rarely acknowledged this. However, Olympic success led to greater publicity for successful female athletes. In 1956 Gillian Sheen won a gold medal in fencing and in 1964 Mary Rand won the first ever gold medal in athletics by a British woman. However, up to the end of the twentieth century, women were still prevented from competing in many Olympic events including bobsleigh, ice hockey, baseball, boxing, football and wrestling. They could not compete in the 1500 metres freestyle, even though women held all the records for long-distance swimming.

Women did begin to take part in sports like rugby and horseracing, which had, up to the 1970s, been exclusively for men. This was due both to increased leisure time and a changing view of women's role in society. In 1991 the first women's rugby world cup was held in Britain; in 1997 the first legal boxing bout between two women was held in Whitland in West Wales.

SOURCE A

Sport has always been a traditionally masculine area, one of the ways in which men have kept themselves apart from women in general and wives and families in particular. Both playing and watching sport has been mainly for men.

Tony Mason, historian, writing in his general history book, Association Football and English Society 1863–1915 *(1980)*

SOURCE B

Any male chauvinists who come to scoff will remain to cheer after 10 minutes. It only takes that long for men to realise that we are serious. They come in with a lot of misconceptions. They soon see things differently. Women players have a lot of skill and they train harder than many men. Their fitness level is superb.

Alice Cooper, press officer for the Women's Rugby World Cup, speaking to the Guardian *newspaper (1991)*

Sally Gunnell on her way to winning a gold medal at the 1992 Olympics in Barcelona

Yet leading women athletes were still paid less than men. Olympic champion hurdler Sally Gunnell threatened not to run in 1993 unless she received the same pay as male athlete Linford Christie. In the end she was paid only half of what he earned. There are still problems with funding sport for women and there has been little change in the coverage of women's sports in the media, especially newer sports.

SOURCE D

Unless you're a tennis player or a golfer you're on a hiding to nothing to get sponsorship or publicity. I can't remember a time when I've picked up a paper and it's been all about women's sport on the back page – it doesn't happen. Any type of publicity is better than none, but right now women's sport comes way below even amateur men's.

Jayne Ludlow, former Wales football captain, speaking in the Western Mail *(August 2010)*

Women still take less part in sport than men. This is partly because of less free time. In 2000 it was estimated that women in full-time work had an average of 12 hours less free time a week than men, often because they undertook a greater share of housework, shopping and child care. Other factors played a part:
● Lack of confidence, encouragement and positive role models;
● Lack of financial and social independence.

SOURCE E

A report by the Women in Sport Foundation found that girls as young as six and seven are already dropping out of sport because they didn't want to look sweaty and unfeminine. Forty per cent of girls have quit any form of sport by the age of 18 while women are 32% less likely to participate in sport than men. A shortage of sporting role models doesn't help. Dazzling icons like Kelly Holmes and Dame Tanni Grey-Thompson have inspired a generation of young women, but many more elite sportswomen fail to reach household name status in a media that devotes just 5% of its back pages coverage to female sport. It would be interesting to compare that figure with the average number of column inches that Cheryl Cole attracts on a weekly basis.

Caroline Hitt, columnist in the Western Mail *newspaper, writing in an article on young women and sport (2008)*

TASKS

1. Why are the following years milestones in participation in top class sport by women: 1956, 1964, 1991 and 1997?

2. What are the major obstacles to women taking part in sport?

3. How useful is Source E to an historian studying the participation of women in sport?

4. How important is media coverage in encouraging participation in sport by women?

5. How far does Source E support the view expressed in Source D?

Growth in organized junior sports

Another feature of sporting participation that changed greatly in the later twentieth century was the growth in organized junior sport. A variety of organizations for young people began to see the benefit of offering a greater range of sports and leisure activities. Youth clubs and scouting and guiding associations offered coaching and training. National youth movements such as Urdd Gobaith Cymru and the Young Farmers Clubs introduced sports competitions into their festivals.

Both the Urdd and Young Farmers hold sporting competitions for their members

The most recent activities have been the May games. The rounders team bust a gut and came a well placed third, with the hockey team also winning. The boys competed in the rugby competition and triumphed and will go on to represent the County at the Royal Welsh Show. All members competing in the athletics did brilliantly and deserve a huge well done.

From the annual report of the Pontfaen Young Farmers Club in Mid Wales (2007)

Although all schools continued to teach physical education and run teams in many sports, the number of matches played between schools declined and Saturday games had seriously declined by the late 1980s. Into the breach stepped local sports clubs in sports like football, hockey, cricket and rugby, who started to coach and organize junior and mini sides at a variety of ages and usually for both boys and girls. The emphasis was largely on developing skills and providing enjoyment.

- There are 28 clubs registered with the League for season 2009/10
- That's a total of 170 teams
- Of which there are 19 girls teams
- And that's a LOT of children playing football each week!!

From the Did You Know section of the Wrexham and District Youth Football League brochure

TASKS

1. Find out why the number of organized school sport fixtures declined in the 1980s.

2. Use Source A and your own knowledge to describe how youth organizations have tried to encourage young people to take part in sport.

3. How important have local sports clubs been in providing sports activities for young people?

4. Find out how many local sports clubs offer activities for young people. How long have they been doing this?

Spectator sport

By the 1960s the condition of many older football grounds was a danger to spectators. In 1985 over 50 fans died in a fire at Bradford City's rundown stadium. Elsewhere, clubs had responded to crowd control issues by putting up barriers on terraces to stop fans getting on to the pitch. In 1989, 95 Liverpool fans died when they were crushed against crowd barriers at the Hillsborough Stadium in Sheffield. A report on the disaster in 1990 led to calls for stadiums of this size to be converted to all-seating. There was more investment in new sports stadiums. Football clubs like Derby County, Sunderland, Swansea and Cardiff have built new **all-seater stadiums** in the last 20 years while others like Newcastle, Manchester United and Chelsea have all carried out major improvements.

I am delighted with the stadium; I never anticipated it would be such a success. The compliments that have been paid from people both in and out of the game are that it has a warm and friendly feel. From my youth I only remember this area as railway sidings and a municipal tip and what has happened to Pride Park is wonderful for Derby. I still get a buzz when I arrive for a home game – it's a dramatic sight, a true county landmark.

Lionel Pickering, chairman of Derby County Football Club, in an interview for the Derby Evening Telegraph *newspaper (2004)*

Parc y Scarlets rugby ground in Llanelli, opened in 2008

In Wales, the hallowed turf of the National Stadium was dug up and auctioned off in 1997. The stadium was demolished to make way for a new Millennium Stadium to host the 1999 Rugby World Cup final. Rugby regions like the Scarlets and the Ospreys built or moved to new grounds in the first 10 years of the twenty-first century. These grounds make the experience for the spectator very different from what it would have been in the years between the wars.

THE INFLUENCE OF TELEVISION AND SPONSORSHIP IN THE LATE TWENTIETH CENTURY

The impact of live television coverage

Television coverage has been highly influential in all aspects of sport in the later part of the twentieth century. This is most marked at the top professional level, but it has also affected playing and watching sport at lower levels. Many social historians would argue that the impact of television coverage has changed many sports out of all recognition compared to what they were like 40 or 50 years ago.

By the early 1960s television was reaching the majority of British households. A situation was developing in which sport was helping make television and television was helping make sport. This alliance was encouraged by the growing interest in sport by major sponsors as a form of advertising.

Mark McCormack, a leading sports promoter, speaking in a television interview (1992)

Television companies have been able to change many 'traditional' sports. For instance, by the 1990s top-level football was no longer played just on Saturday afternoons: the viewer could watch televised football on most weekdays.

SOURCE B

Day	Broadcaster	Kick off	Tournament
Saturday	BSkyB	12 pm	FA Premier League
Saturday	BSkyB	5.30 pm	Scottish Premier League
Saturday	BSkyB	8.30 pm	Italian League
Sunday	ITV	2 pm	Football League
Sunday	BSkyB	4 pm	FA Premier League
Sunday	BSkyB	8 pm	Spanish League
Monday	BSkyB	8 pm	FA Premier League
Tuesday	ITV	7.45 pm	Football League
Thursday	ITV	7.45 pm	Football League

Typical television coverage of football in a week in 2001

Cricket used to be a game played quietly between two teams wearing white. Since the coming of satellite TV, players in one-day matches have worn colourful kits and games have been floodlit, with players walking to the wicket to the sound of pop music. The 20-20 version of the game is ideal for broadcasting on television, as it is relatively quick, entertaining and someone always wins.

TV companies have also brought viewers a whole new range of sports as entertainment, increasing the profile of sports like American football and basketball. **Satellite and cable channels** even helped create new sports like beach volleyball and competitive skydiving.

TV has made one-time minority sports very popular. *Pot Black* was a minor BBC2 programme when it began in the late 1960s to coincide with the growth of colour television. It began to attract large audiences and soon the world snooker championships were being covered live from the Crucible Theatre in Sheffield. The game became compulsive watching for many people and snooker players like Steve Davies became rich sporting superstars.

SOURCE C

A modern cricket match played in coloured kit

SOURCE D

Steve is attempting to pot the pink ball, and for those of you who are watching on black and white television, the pink ball is next to the green.

Ted Lowe, commentator on the snooker show Pot Black, *trying to be helpful to viewers (1970)*

Similarly darts changed from a pub entertainment to a world sport, making household names of players like Eric Bristow and Jocky Wilson. Television coverage made the London Marathon an essential part of the sporting calendar by bringing it to a live TV audience. Ice hockey also gained from TV exposure, with the Cardiff Devils regularly winning the League and Cup competitions in the sport.

However, not every sport has benefited from television coverage. For example, netball is played in almost every secondary school in Britain. In Australia, South Africa and New Zealand, the national teams are sponsored and the sport is seen regularly on TV. But in Britain it has failed to get the TV exposure that would lead to increased popularity and sponsorship, leaving it a minority sport. The fact that it is a female sport may be an issue.

Many people think of ice hockey as a small sport but TV coverage has helped to raise attendances of 17,000 and 10,000 in Manchester and Sheffield, which are larger than many football league crowds. When our product is in demand internationally, we'll be looking to sell that product around the world. Sky's investment will not guarantee our success, but it will put us in the best position to negotiate when it happens.

An Ice Hockey Superleague spokesman, speaking on the BBC news in 1999

Competing television channels

The growth of televised sport since the 1970s has been enormous. The terrestrial monopoly of BBC and ITV has been broken by satellite and cable coverage.

Satellite links can now relay television pictures around the world with live images being shown as they happen. Gaining television rights to sporting events is big business, with companies paying millions of pounds for the rights to screen certain popular sports and events.

	1983	1985	1986	1988	1992	1997
Length of contract (yrs)	2	0.5	2	4	5	4
Broadcaster	BBC/ITV	BBC	BBC/ITV	ITV	BSkyB	BSkyB
Rights fee (£m)	5.2	1.3	6.3	44	191.5	670
Annual rights fee (£m)	2.6	2.6	3.1	11	38.3	167.5
Number of live matches per season	10	6	14	18	60	60
Fees per live match (£m)	0.26	0.43	0.22	0.61	0.64	2.79

Official Premier League figures showing financial deals between television companies and English footballing bodies 1983–1997

There is little doubt that the competition between the television providers has been of great financial benefit to sport. Satellite television companies, such as Sky Television, have dedicated sports channels and they continue to provide coverage of sport to those subscribers with a satellite receiver. They have also developed the idea of 'pay to watch', where viewers with satellite dishes have had to pay extra in order to receive live coverage of a football match or a boxing bout. The UK government has been very concerned over the growth of subscription based television and has identified certain sports that have to be available on free to view television channels.

The Olympic Games, the Football World Cup, the European Football Championships, the FA Cup final, the Scottish Cup final (in Scotland), the Grand National, the Wimbledon tennis finals, the Rugby World Cup final, the Derby, the rugby league Challenge Cup final.

The so-called 'sporting crown jewels', which must appear on free-to-air TV, as established in 1998

The impact of television coverage on sport

There is no doubt that the relationship between television and sport, particularly at the top level, has progressed so that the two are financially dependent on each other.

There are some positive advantages to this relationship, but there are also some disadvantages. Social historians and commentators have argued for many years over the relationship between television and sport.

Positive impacts of television on sport	Negative impacts of television on sport
1. Television promotes the positive image of sport.	1. Television shows the bad behaviour of certain stars.
2. Television allows fans to watch their favourite sporting events from their own homes.	2. There is excessive coverage of some sports so that fans are not encouraged to attend events.
3. Television has popularised sport, especially minority sports.	3. Television has changed the rules of many sports and the timing of sporting events.
4. Television has created income to invest in sports development.	4. Too much television money stays at the higher levels of the sports.
5. Television has developed new technology to improve viewing and confirm decisions by officials.	5. In some sports, television replays undermine confidence in officials

The televising of football in Britain has generated vast sums of money for the sport not only from deals for television rights but also from the sponsorship opportunities that greater coverage of the sport has provided. This influx of capital has arguably allowed football, for example, to improve many aspects of the game including the stadia, professionalism in performance and staging of events, and provided new resources to support grassroots developments.

G. Whannel and J. Williams, sports lecturers, writing in The Rise of Satellite Television, *published in Sociology Review (1993)*

We have now reached a stage where sport at the top level has become completely show business with everything that one associates with show business – the cult of the individual, high salaries, the desire to present the game as a spectacle. This has meant more money, less sportsmanship and more emphasis on winning. All this has come about because of the huge influence of television.

Dennis Fellowes, Chairman of the British Olympic Association, speaking in 1983

1. Some historians claim that television coverage has changed some sports out of all recognition. Do you agree?

2. How useful is Source B to an historian studying the impact of television on sport in the last 20 years?

3. How has television affected minority sports like snooker and darts?

4. Compare the impact that television has had on sports like ice hockey and netball.

5. What does Source F tell you about the money provided by television channels?

6. Explain why competition between television channels has been of benefit to the development of sport.

7. Draw up a balance sheet to compare the positive and negative impacts of television on sport.

8. Look at Sources H and I. Why do they say different things about the impact of television on sport?

Sponsorship and its impact on the development of sport

It can be argued that the other major factor that has affected sport has been the growth in **sponsorship**. Companies want to be associated with sport because the television exposure helps to sell their products.

Serious sports sponsorship in Britain began in 1957 when the brewing company Whitbread offered £6,000 in prize money to sponsor the Ascot Gold Cup. This initial investment soon became replicated everywhere. As the century progressed, tournaments and competitions, kit and equipment, teams and players were all sponsored. In the 1990s the League of Wales had football clubs called Inter CableTel and Total Network Solutions while Birmingham Rugby Club became Pertemps Bees for a number of seasons. By the end of the century sports clubs were entering sponsorship deals to build new grounds like the Ricoh Arena in Coventry and Arsenal's Emirates stadium.

Mars and Flora, who wanted their products to be associated with energy and health, sponsored the London Marathon. Companies paid huge sums of money to link their products with winners. Stars like Roger Federer, Tiger Woods, Lewis Hamilton and Gary Lineker became very wealthy through sponsorship and advertising.

SOURCE A

A sponsored football shirt from the 2010/11 season

SOURCE B

Sponsoring a team or sporting event can give your company a real boost. By sponsoring a local team, your company's logo will appear on the jerseys worn by the team. Your company's name will be on banners posted at matches, as well as in promotional material about upcoming events. You may also be eligible for free tickets to events, which in turn can be used to reward customers or your employees.

Jenny McCune, a financial adviser, writing in a guide to sponsorship (2002)

Sponsorship has transformed modern sport. The commercial side of sport is, these days, so much on display. Whether it is corporate hospitality at Wimbledon, Test cricketers wondering whether the new Indian Premier League (IPL) will transform their sport (and their bank balances), or Premiership footballers signing lucrative deals for the new season, money clearly matters in sporting life.

Chris Bowlby, a BBC journalist, writing in the BBC History Magazine in an article called The Link between Sport and Money *(2008)*

It is not only the major professional sports that have benefited from sponsorship. Most semi-professional and amateur sporting clubs and organizations couldn't survive without the valuable support offered by local companies who will sponsor kit, equipment, and matches and take out advertisements in match programmes.

CLEMENTS DECOR CENTRE

Main Stockists of Sikkens & Sadolin.
10,000 Paint colours available from stock
in Crown, Dulux and Macpherson.

Suppliers of
decorating materials to
**Aberystwyth Town
Football Club**

37 Cambrian Street
Aberystwyth SY23 1NZ
Telephone : 01970 612513
Fax : 01970 611013

An advertisement from a sponsor in a match day
programme for Aberystwyth Town FC

TASKS

1. Give examples of sponsorship in sport over the last 50 years.

2. Use Source B and your own knowledge to explain why companies often want to sponsor sport.

3. How useful is Source C to an historian studying the sponsorship of sport?

4. Collect examples of businesses that sponsor sport in your local area.

5. Discuss the following view: 'Sponsorship has had more influence on the development of sport over the last 25 years than anything else – including television.'

CONTROVERSY IN SPORT

Sport has had an influence on many issues that concern wider society.

Sport and politics

Politicians and leaders have always used sport and sporting events for political purposes. The high international profile of the Olympic Games has always offered ways to use sport for **propaganda** and for making political points. A good example was seen in the 1936 Olympic Games in Berlin with Adolf Hitler's Nazi regime ruling Germany. The Olympics gave Hitler a unique opportunity to show the world the supposed superiority of the Aryan race. Leni Riefenstahl's famous film of the events shows all the German sporting successes together with the Nazi pomp and propaganda. Nationalism and politics had entered the Olympics in a major way. Unfortunately for Hitler, the black American athlete Jesse Owens was the star performer. In the new 100,000 seater stadium, he won four gold medals – 100 m, 200 m, long jump and sprint relay – setting a new Olympic record in each. An outraged Hitler refused to attend the presentation ceremony.

Jesse Owens at the 1936 Olympic Games

At the Mexico Olympic Games in 1968, American sprinters Tommie Smith and John Carlos used the **medal ceremony** to show their support for the Black Power movement. As well as their famous gloved salute, the two US athletes received their medals shoeless, but wearing black socks, to represent black poverty. Smith wore a black scarf around his neck to represent black pride and Carlos wore a necklace of beads, which he said were for those black people that had been lynched, tarred and feathered or killed.

US athletes Tommie Smith and John Carlos performing their Black Power salute at the 1968 Summer Olympics in Mexico City

If I win, I am American, not a black American. But if I did something bad, then they would say I am a Negro. We are black and we are proud of being black. Black America will understand what we did tonight.

Tommie Smith, being interviewed on the Grandstand television programme after he had received his gold medal (1968)

Sport entered the political arena at the Olympics again during the Cold War period. The 1980 Games were held in Moscow, in the Soviet Union for the first time. The United States and 64 other countries **boycotted** the games because of the Soviet invasion of Afghanistan. Fifteen other countries marched in the opening ceremony with the Olympic flag instead of with their national flags, and the Olympic flag and Olympic hymn were used at medal ceremonies when athletes from these countries won medals. In response to this boycott, fourteen Communist countries including the Soviet Union, Cuba and East Germany boycotted the 1984 Games in Los Angeles in the USA. The Soviet Union explained its decision referring to security concerns and an anti-Soviet hysteria being whipped up in the United States.

On a more positive note, the 1995 Rugby World Cup was held in South Africa. The South African government, and President Nelson Mandela in particular, was able to use the tournament as an opportunity to show the world that the country was united and making progress as a nation after the apartheid era.

President Nelson Mandela congratulating Francois Pienaar after South Africa had won the Rugby World Cup in 1995

A memorial stone and panel at the site of the Munich Olympic Park in memory of the Israeli athletes killed during the 1972 Olympic Games

Terrorism

Unfortunately the high profile of sporting events has also encouraged the activities of terrorists. The most infamous attack came in the 1972 Olympic Games at Munich. Early in the morning on September 5, 1972, eight members of the Palestinian terrorist organization, Black September, raided the accommodation of the Israeli athletics team. Two Israeli athletes were killed during the raid and nine others were taken hostage. After spending most of the day trying to negotiate the release of Palestinian prisoners in Israel in exchange for the hostages,

the Black September members finally realised that their demands were not going to be met. They then asked for transport to an airport and two planes to take them to Egypt. The German authorities planned a rescue attempt at the airport. Unfortunately, the rescue attempt failed and all nine of the Israeli hostages were killed during the shoot-out. Five of the Black September members were also killed. Israel responded to the massacre with a series of airstrikes and killings of those suspected of planning the attacks.

The murder of the Israeli athletes at Munich altered the nature and extent of sports event security forever. At every major international sporting event held since the 1972 Olympics, security has been a significant and highly visible presence. In addition to on-site protection, the police forces seek and obtain information with respect to any possible terrorist risk that might manifest itself.

Charles Bierbauer, an American sports reporter, speaking in a radio broadcast in 1996

Athletes and sports officials have been frequent targets of threats, kidnappings and assassination attempts. The Iraqi taekwondo team was driving to a training camp in neighbouring Jordan in May 2006, when their convoy was stopped about 70 miles west of Baghdad. None of the 15 athletes was seen alive again, but thirteen of their bodies were found a year later in the desert. One of the more recent terrorist attacks occurred at a cricket tournament in Pakistan. Masked gunmen attacked the Sri Lankan team as they travelled in their team bus outside a stadium in Lahore. Seven people were killed in the attack and six of the Sri Lankan cricket players were wounded. In January 2010, separatist gunmen opened fire on the coach carrying Togo's national football squad to the African Cup of Nations in Angola, killing the driver and wounding nine others, including two players.

SOURCE G

The resumption of Test cricket will not take place in Pakistan until security against attacks can be restored. And in a nation that cherishes the sport as a second religion, the thinking is that the demand for such from millions of Pakistani cricket enthusiasts will be loud and strong. And someday, in the hopefully not too distant future, the terrorists will regret the day they decided to reintroduce their murderous ways to the world of sport.

An editorial in the Sunday Paper, *an on-line newspaper (2009)*

TASKS

1. Explain why politicians have always tried to show an interest in sport and sporting events.

2. Carry out a case study of a sporting occasion that has been used to make political points.

3. What does Source B tell you about the connection between sport and politics?

4. How useful is Source D to an historian studying the relationship between politics and sport?

5. Describe the terrorist attack that took place in the 1972 Munich Olympics.

6. Explain why terrorists have often targeted sporting events.

Drug abuse in sport

At the top level, sport is now far removed from the days of amateur competition. Elite athletes can earn millions of pounds every year in prize and appearance money, and millions more in sponsorship and endorsements. The lure of success is great and unfortunately some athletes have used illegal drugs to improve performance.

The use of **performance enhancing drugs** is on record as early as the 1904 Olympics, when Thomas Hicks won the marathon after receiving an injection of strychnine in the middle of the race. The first official ban on 'stimulating substances' by a sporting organization was introduced by the International Amateur Athletic Federation in 1928. However, despite the health risks, and despite the regulating bodies' attempts to eliminate drugs from sport, the use of illegal substances to improve performance continued to rise during the twentieth century.

Anti-drug work was complicated in the 1970s and 1980s by suspicions of state-sponsored drug use being encouraged in some countries. One of the countries suspected was the former German Democratic Republic (East Germany). In the 1968 Olympics, the country won 9 gold medals; in 1972 it was 20; in 1976 it had risen to 40. These suspicions over drug use by athletes have now been largely proven.

Drug cheats are regularly identified and banned. However, the penalties for cheating often seem small. A six-month or one-year ban from competition seems a small penalty to pay for further years of sporting and financial success.

Ben Johnson of Canada raises his hand in victory during the 1988 Olympic Games 100 m final. Johnson was later disqualified for drug use

It had been a hard race but not terribly hard. He went into the shower first, took his jersey off and put six tablets on the table. He used to keep them wrapped in foil. I'm in bed, waiting to shower, he comes out and one has fallen on the floor. He accused me of taking it. 'Where's my stuff? If you want stuff, ask me, don't steal it.' He scrabbled on the floor and it was under a table. It had dropped off and rolled underneath. He was sorry about it. 'I'm glad you don't need this stuff,' he said.

Colin Lewis, roommate of cyclist Tommy Simpson in 1967, interviewed for the book, Put Me Back on My Bike: In Search of Tom Simpson *(2002)*

SOURCE C

Name	Year	Sport	Offence	Punishment
Tommy Simpson	1967	Cycling	Using amphetamines	None but he died in a race
Ben Johnson	1988	Athletics	Taking anabolic steroids	2 year ban
Diego Maradona	1991	Football	Using cocaine	15 month ban
Michelle Smith	1996	Swimming	Tampering with urine samples	4 year ban
Linford Christie	1999	Athletics	Taking nandrolone	2 year ban
Dwain Chambers	2003	Athletics	Using tetrahydrogestrinone	2 year ban
Shane Warne	2003	Cricket	Taking a banned diuretic	1 year ban
Martina Hingis	2007	Tennis	Using cocaine	2 year ban
Marion Jones	2008	Athletics	Taking anabolic steroids	6 months in jail for perjury

Some of the better known scandals involving drug-taking in sport

SOURCE D

I've been in this business for a long time. I know what goes on. And not just me, everyone knows. The riders, the team leaders, the organizers, the officials, the journalists. As a rider you feel tied into this system. It's like being on the motorway. The law says there's a speed limit of 65, but everyone is driving 70 or faster. Why should I be the one who obeys the speed limit? I had two alternatives: either fit in with the others or go back to being a house painter. Who in my situation would have done that?

Alex Zulle, a leading Swiss cyclist, in a police interview following his arrest for drug offences in 1998

At 17, I joined the East Berlin Sports Institute. My speciality was the 80 m hurdles. We swore that we would never speak to anyone about our training methods, including our parents. The training was very hard. We were all watched. One day my trainer advised me to take pills to improve my performance. He told me the pills were vitamins, but I soon had cramp in my legs and my voice became gruff. I started to grow hair on my face and my periods stopped. I then refused to take the pills. One morning in October 1977, the secret police took me at 7 am and questioned me about my refusal to take the pills prescribed by the trainer. I then decided to flee to the West, with my fiancé.

Renate Neufeld, an East German athlete who fled to West Germany in 1977,
giving evidence to an enquiry into drug testing (2000)

TASKS

1. Explain why drug taking by athletes increased in the late twentieth century.

2. How far does Source B support the view that drug taking was common in some sport by the 1960s?

3. Look at Source C. Investigate two of the high profile drug scandals in the table.

4. Look at Sources D and E. Do the sources support each other in their views on why athletes take drugs?

This section provides guidance on how to answer question 1(c) from Units 1 and 2. It is a source analysis and evaluation question, which is linked to the recall of your own knowledge. It is worth 5 marks.

Question 1(c) – extent of support for a viewpoint

How far does Source A support the view that more people participated in sport towards the end of the twentieth century? [5 marks]

SOURCE A

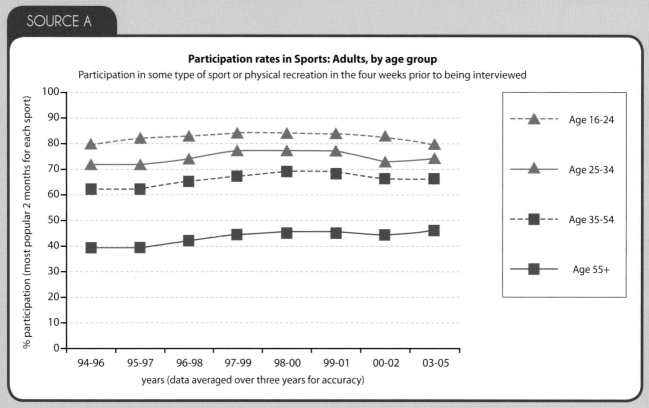

Participation rates in Sports: Adults, by age group
Participation in some type of sport or physical recreation in the four weeks prior to being interviewed

From an official report into sport and health in Scotland, published by the Scottish Government in 2006

Tips on how to answer

This question can relate to a visual or a written source.

- If it is a visual source you should aim to **pick out relevant details** from what you can see in the illustration and, equally importantly, from the caption that accompanies the source. It is useful to scribble notes around the source.
- If it is a written source you should **underline or highlight** the key points.
- You should bring in your **own knowledge** of this topic to expand upon these points and to provide additional material that is not provided in the source.
- You should use this material to show how the content and the attribution helps to support the viewpoint (or not).
- To obtain maximum marks you must remember to give a **reasoned judgement** that addresses the question. E.g. 'This source does/does not support the view that … because …'

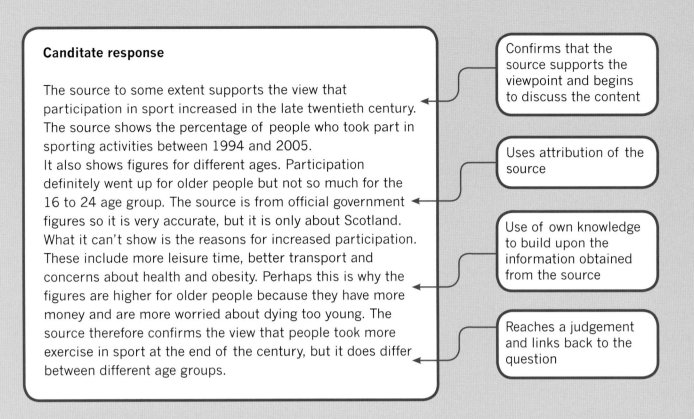

Canditate response

The source to some extent supports the view that participation in sport increased in the late twentieth century. The source shows the percentage of people who took part in sporting activities between 1994 and 2005. It also shows figures for different ages. Participation definitely went up for older people but not so much for the 16 to 24 age group. The source is from official government figures so it is very accurate, but it is only about Scotland. What it can't show is the reasons for increased participation. These include more leisure time, better transport and concerns about health and obesity. Perhaps this is why the figures are higher for older people because they have more money and are more worried about dying too young. The source therefore confirms the view that people took more exercise in sport at the end of the century, but it does differ between different age groups.

Confirms that the source supports the viewpoint and begins to discuss the content

Uses attribution of the source

Use of own knowledge to build upon the information obtained from the source

Reaches a judgement and links back to the question

Examiner's comment

A developed answer that makes good use of the figures. The candidate expands upon the content of the source, explaining key details and supplies background knowledge to illustrate them, e.g. the possible reasons for increased participation. A clear attempt has been made to use the information in the source to answer the question. This is an informed and reasoned answer with a supported judgement linked directly to the question. It is worthy of maximum [5] marks.

Now you have a go

SOURCE B

A photograph of Prime Minister Tony Blair with his wife Cherie and footballer David Beckham. They were at a meeting in 2005 to announce the venue for the 2012 Olympics, which was given to London

Question

How far does Source B support the view that politicians have increasingly become involved in sport and sporting events?
[5 marks]

CHAPTER 4

WHAT KINDS OF ENTERTAINMENT WERE INFLUENTIAL IN PEOPLE'S LIVES IN WALES AND ENGLAND UP TO 1945?

PEOPLE'S ENTERTAINMENT

For those with enough time and money, there were many types of entertainment on offer. While the very wealthy rarely took part in any of the entertainments that follow, they were popular with the other classes, in varying degrees. Many people also made their own entertainment: pianos were quite common in many households and also in public houses.

Theatres and music halls

Most large towns had at least one theatre and several music halls. The theatre or the music hall provided a welcome break and, for many people, a visit was a special treat.

By 1900 most theatres were comfortable and some were even luxurious. These tended to be frequented more by middle class visitors. Crowds flocked to hear the operettas of Gilbert and Sullivan such as *HMS Pinafore* and *The Mikado*. The plays of George Bernard Shaw were also very popular. Music halls had grown in popularity in Victorian towns and cities and were more popular with working people. Entertainers like Marie Lloyd and Harry Lauder were very well known. A visit to a music hall tended to be more raucous than a visit to the theatre. The crowd would laugh and sing along with the entertainers who could be quite suggestive in their acts.

Several commentators at the time were concerned over the poor behaviour of crowds at some music hall venues.

SOURCE A

The audience in the music hall is not a distinguished-looking one but the vast majority are respectable. You will see little family parties – father, mother, and perhaps a grown-up daughter or a child or two – and most of them are probably regular visitors… Then there are several girls with their sweethearts, while the rest of the audience is made up of young men, the local "bloods," who have a fashion in some districts of wearing a cigar behind the ear. Taken as a whole, the audience is not remarkable for intelligence; it is perfectly happy listening to dull songs, corny jokes and romantic rubbish.

F. Anstey, an American theatre critic writing an article called 'London Music Halls', Harper's New Monthly Magazine, *1891*

Music halls were important in the development of entertainment. In particular, they offered songs with hooks or catchy choruses. Dance bands and show musicals in the 1930s and the writers of the early pop songs in the 1950s and 1960s inherited these features.

Social activities in churches and chapels

Many people attended church and chapel regularly at the start of the twentieth century. In Wales in particular, in the early twentieth century there was a movement known as the Revival, which encouraged many more people to attend a place of worship. This greatly boosted attendance at chapels in particular.

Sunday was the day of worship, but churches and chapels also organized leisure activities all week and all year. Activities connected with churches and chapels included:

- Choirs;
- Brass bands;
- Drama groups;
- Eisteddfodau;
- *Cymanfaoedd Canu;*
- Penny readings;
- Sporting teams.

For many people, especially women and children and in rural areas, the activities organized by the local church or chapel provided their only regular form of entertainment.

These activities were also very important in keeping the language and culture of Wales alive. People loved having the chance to sing, write, act and play. A **Cymanfa Ganu** was a singing festival, and in 1906 nearly 300 *Cymanfaoedd Canu* were held across Wales.

SOURCE B

Zoar Chapel, Merthyr Tydfil
Thursday, March 20th, 1930
To commence at 7.30pm

**PROGRAMME
Of
Miscellaneous Concert**

ARTISTES
Soprano:
Miss ELSIE SUDDARY, London
(Three Choirs Festival and London and Provincial Concerts)

Tenor:
Mr TOM PICKERING, Mus. Bac. Wales
(London and Provincial Concerts)

THE ZOAR CHORAL SOCIETY
Organist and Conductor:
Mr D. T. Davies, A.R.C.O., L.R.A.M.
(Organist and Conductor of Zoar Chapel)

Proceeds in aid of Zoar Chapel Funds

The *Cymanfa Ganu* remained a distinctive feature of Welsh life throughout most of the next century. Churches and chapels were also strong supporters of the cultural festivals known as Eisteddfodau. Eisteddfodau had their roots deep in Welsh history, but they were revived in the nineteenth century and had become a mass form of entertainment in Wales. There were National Eisteddfodau where the standard of singing, playing and literature was of the highest quality, but for most people in Welsh communities, hardly a week would go by without a local church, chapel or other organization holding a local eisteddfod. The eisteddfod movement survived most of the pressures of the twentieth century and still remains an essential part of entertainment for many people in Wales and beyond.

Choirs and brass bands were often associated with churches

SOURCE C

Tabernacle Choir, Llandovery, 1898

and chapels, but these were actually more community based. Many small villages and towns had their male voice choirs and these regularly entered competitions and held concerts, which many people attended. Local employers as well as places of worship often supported brass bands. In South Wales, the Parc and Dare Band and the Cory Band became famous and provided entertainment for many people.

Pubs and institutes

Throughout Wales and England at the start of the twentieth century, various organizations continued to do their best to keep workers out of public houses and away from the dangers of alcohol. The public houses were increasingly opposed by many people for a number of different reasons: wives worrying about their husbands' heavy drinking, chapel goers worrying about moral standards and industrial masters worrying about absence from work. The **Temperance movement** was founded in the nineteenth century and campaigned against consumption of alcohol. Other organizations dedicated to this included the Band of Hope and the Rechabites.

SOURCE D

The St. David's branch of the Good Templars temperance society

However, for many workers, visits to the pub or club were an essential part of their leisure time. This was generally seen as a male activity. Most working men also had their own clubs or institutes, which were funded by and open to members. Besides alcohol and company, pubs and clubs also offered a range of entertainments. Sports teams used them as headquarters and the institutes in particular had facilities such as billiard rooms, concert halls and libraries. In the slate quarrying areas of North Wales, the Caban fulfilled the same function.

SOURCE E

The Caban wasn't just a canteen. It was also a concert hall, a theatre and an eisteddfod pavilion! Over lunch the quarrymen entertained one another by singing hymns, folk songs and cerdd dant, reciting poetry and passages from the Bible, and miming and acting. General knowledge quizzes and spelling competitions were very popular, and there were always loud arguments about religion and politics.

Geraint Jenkins, an historian, writing in the textbook Wales, Yesterday and Today *(1990)*

SOURCE F

An example of an institute, the newly built Newbridge Memorial Hall (1908)

Because they did not have their own clubhouses many of the early rugby and football clubs would have been founded, met and even changed before matches in a local public house. If anything rivalled sport in popular activity and entertainment at the time, it was the 'pub'. Most villages, especially in industrialised areas, had a tremendous number of public houses and beer-shops per head of the population, and before licensing laws were introduced they were open for the greater part of the day.

David Egan, an historian writing in the textbook Coal Society *(1987)*

TASKS

1. How useful is Source A to an historian studying the popular music halls of the early twentieth century?

2. Use Sources B and C and your own knowledge to explain why churches and chapels were important in providing leisure activities for people.

3. How far does Source G support the view that pubs were the most popular place for entertainment in the early years of the century?

THE IMPACT OF THE CINEMA

The popularity of the silent cinema

Film – the first of the mass media – was invented towards the end of the nineteenth century. In the early years of the twentieth century, films were a novelty shown in music halls and at fairs. William Haggar, who made more than 30 films, showed these around South and West Wales in travelling tents called **Bioscopes** with their own generators and organs.

The first proper cinema in Britain opened in Balham in London in 1907. The first purpose-built cinema in Wales was the Carlton in Swansea. It was built in 1914, by which time there were over 4,000 cinemas in Britain. They were often called 'Living Pictures' or 'Picture Palaces' and showed short, silent black and white films, usually accompanied by a pianist. Special Saturday morning screenings, called matinées, were offered to children for about 1 penny entry.

Dramatic serials like *The Perils of Pauline* were very popular. These serials sometimes had cliff-hanger endings, which guaranteed an audience for the next episode. The comedy films of Charlie Chaplin also attracted big audiences after 1914. Film particularly appealed to working-class people and was sometimes mocked as the 'poor man's theatre'. Even in its early days, there were critics who were concerned about the negative influence that 'the pictures' could have on the behaviour of people, especially the young.

The first thing I can remember about the cinema on the square was that it was like a fairground with an organ and marionettes or whatever they were. It had a huge marquee. It had been raining and you had duckboards underfoot. The only thing I remember vividly – why I don't know – was this Red Indian crawling up this brook or stream and chasing somebody and he had a huge dagger in his mouth. I can see him now.

Trevor Davies, remembering his first visit to the cinema as a seven year old in 1907. This was in an interview for a book on the history of the cinema in Wales

At Swansea Quarter Sessions on Friday last 'penny horribles' and bioscope pictures of burglaries were said to have influenced two youths in committing a number of burglaries and stealing jewellery. Detective Sergeant Howard said that the boys had seen bioscope pictures of a burglary and they stole a revolver and dagger to arm themselves like the hero of the pictures.

Taken from a report in the magazine The Bioscope *(October 1908)*

A poster advertising the silent film series,
The Perils of Pauline *(1914)*

Many cinemas up to 1920 were hastily built 'flea pits'. They had hard wooden seats, noisy audiences and unreliable projectors. Despite this, the years after 1920 saw the cinema become one of the most popular forms of entertainment. The cinema offered an escape from the harsh realities of working life and provided good quality entertainment for every generation. Attendance figures for British cinemas soared.

As the Park cinema was in a zinc building, one clever chap said that he would get in without paying if he had a tin opener! The disadvantage of the zinc cinema was that it was at the mercy of the weather. It was so noisy when the rain banged on the roof and in the summer the place was like an oven.

Emyr Owen, remembering the Parc cinema in Blaenau Ffestiniog as it was in the 1920s. This was reported in an article in a local paper in the early 1960s after the cinema closed

I think it cost 1/9d (8p) to go to the Empire and 2/3d (11p) to sit in the gallery of the Majestic. You would feel like a lord. There was a café lounge in the Majestic and if you were seen there you were really something.

John Williams of Caernarfon speaking about the town's cinemas in the 1930s. He was interviewed by his granddaughter for a school project in 1999

As the popularity of the cinema grew in the 1920s, so did the level of investment. More cinemas became warm and luxurious 'dream palaces'. Even their names reeked of luxury: the Empire, the Paramount, the Majestic, the Royal. The piano had been replaced by the sound of the Wurlitzer organ. The quality of films improved with the big cinema companies, MGM, Fox and Warner Brothers dominating the industry from their Hollywood studios. The silent comedies of Charlie Chaplin, featuring his famous character the Tramp, remained popular, as did the antics of Buster Keaton, the romantic films of Rudolph Valentino and the historical epics of Cecil B. de Mille. One famous British star of the 1920s was Ivor Novello, who was born in Cardiff.

TASKS

1. What do Sources A, B and C tell you about silent cinemas and films at this time?

2. Describe the development of cinemas in the 1920s.

3. How far does Source D support the view that early cinemas were often uncomfortable places?

4. Use Source E and your own knowledge to explain why cinemas became more popular in the 1920s.

5. Use the Internet to find out how many cinemas existed in your area in the 1920s.

The golden age of cinema-going

Films remained silent until 1927 when audiences heard Al Jolson talking in *The Jazz Singer*. There had been attempts to record sound on film before, but this was the first feature length 'talkie', produced by Warner Brothers using the *Movietone* technique. Suddenly the whole film industry turned to produce '**talkies**'. The entertainment business was never to be the same again and people's lives were to be changed hugely.

Even in the years of economic recession in the late 1920s and 1930s, the cinema remained an incredibly popular and influential form of entertainment. In the 1930s, half the population of Britain went to the cinema at least once a week. Stars like Clark Gable, Errol Flynn and Greta Garbo became famous all round the world. The cinema attracted both young and old. Young people met there, as it became a popular place for dating. Matinées remained for children on Saturday mornings when parents wanted a lie-in or had jobs to do. Some people continued to worry about the impact of the cinema on the morals of young people.

Then the talking pictures came. And it was a sad thing for those who played the piano. I know of one man in the Swansea valley who committed suicide! But for most of us, it was an awfully exciting thing when the talkies came.

Peggy Jones of Brynamman, remembering the coming of the 'talkies' in a radio interview (1978)

O boy, stay away from the dirty cinema!
It's a trap set by Satan of flowers and feathers.
A school of wickedness is the cinema truly;
It kills all goodness which grows in the earth.

Extract from a poem by the Reverend Thomas David Evans of Gwernogle, Carmarthenshire, published in a chapel magazine (1939)

Cinema in Wales

By 1934 Wales had over 320 cinemas. Most large towns had several cinemas, with Cardiff having over 20. Westerns, gangster films, musicals and cartoons provided escapism for people of all ages. In 1935 the first Welsh language talkie, *Y Chwarelwr* (*The Quarryman*), attracted large crowds in North Wales.

Several films about the South Wales mining valleys were made during this period. The sentimental Hollywood film *How Green Was My Valley* showed a romantic view of life in a mining community in South Wales. *Proud Valley* starred black American singer and actor Paul Robeson as a heroic miner who gave his life to save his workmates underground.

In the early 1930s, Sir Ifan ap Owen Edwards was in Portugal where he saw and heard the first film in the Portuguese language. He told a journalist in 1935, "If Portugal could do this, why not Wales?" It was the same ethos and drive that produced *Y Chwarelwr* that led nearly 50 years later to the establishment of S4C, the Welsh language television channel, whose first chief executive was Sir Ifan's son, Owen Edwards.

A view expressed on the website of the National Screen and Sound Archive of Wales (2010)

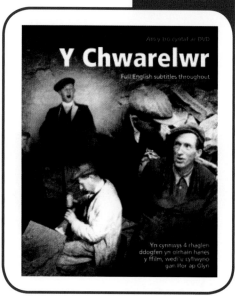

Cover of the re-edited version of Y Chwarelwr (2000)

By permission of The National Library of Wales

The cinema was to have a very large impact on people's lives during the 1930s and beyond. It really did become an important part of the lives of the majority of people: women, men and children.

We'd all be there at the cinema, camped on the doorstop at first light. Milling, jostling, whiling away the time eating bacon sandwiches and sherbet, and generally encouraging the management to open up by breaking a window or two and drawing moustaches on every poster in sight. We didn't really watch the films at all. And we certainly didn't go to hear them. The air was solid with screams, cheers, hisses, boos, insults, which got louder when someone in the balcony climbed high enough to hold his hand in front of the beam of light from the projection box.

A cinema goer from Nottinghamshire who was a teenager in the 1930s, remembering his experiences in a forum on the BBC website (2007)

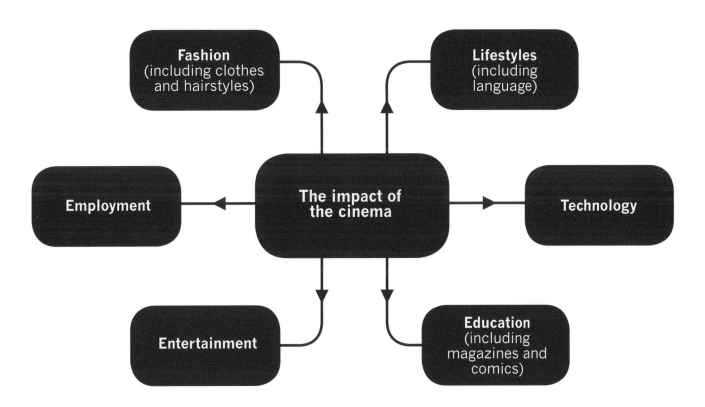

The impact of the cinema

- **Fashion** (including clothes and hairstyles)
- **Lifestyles** (including language)
- **Employment**
- **Technology**
- **Entertainment**
- **Education** (including magazines and comics)

TASKS

1. What does Source F tell you about the arrival of the talkies?

2. Describe the growth of the cinema in Wales in the 1930s.

3. Why do Sources G and J have different views about the cinema in the 1930s?

4. Use Source H and your own knowledge to explain the importance of the film *Y Chwarelwr*.

5. Working in groups, find out more about the impact that the cinema had on people's lives in the 1930s. Then use your research to answer the question:

   Why was cinema important to people's lives in the 1930s?

Cinema during the Second World War

The cinema continued to have a major impact on people's lives during the Second World War. By the time war was declared in September 1939 it was generally accepted that civilian morale was going to play a crucial role in the outcome and cinema would be influential in this.

Cinemas in Britain were closed for a week at the start of the war because the government was worried about the potential disaster of bombs falling on crowded cinemas. However, the realisation soon dawned that visits to the cinema were vital to maintain morale and provide escape and relaxation. Cinemas also provided a way of relaying information, especially to those people who were less likely to read newspapers and information leaflets. A government department, the **Ministry of Information** (MOI), controlled the output of the British film industry. The kind of scripts they approved showed the heroism of British forces and ordinary people and poked fun at the enemy. Popular wartime films included:

- *The Way to the Stars*, about the RAF;
- *Millions Like Us*, about life on the Home Front;
- *Henry V*, Shakespeare's historical play showing England defeating her enemies.

The Hollywood studios continued to pour out big budget movies. People went to enjoy escapist films like the historical epic, *Gone With the Wind*, voted in 2009 to be the most popular film of all time. Other American films were made from an anti-Nazi perspective including *Mrs Miniver*, *Casablanca* and *The Great Dictator* in which Charlie Chaplin mocked Adolf Hitler.

Cinemas were also used to show public information films about topics like air raid drills and blackout precautions. The Ministry of Information was also careful to censor material. Newsreels – news films with a spoken commentary – were carefully edited to take out film that the censors thought was too depressing, such as bomb damage.

During the Second World War, the cinema provided the escape from the harsh realities that people needed. If there was an air raid, a slide would be projected on the screen saying 'Air raid in progress – you may leave the cinema if you so desire.' Very few people did. Cinemas were solidly built and would survive anything but a direct hit.

The average weekly attendance rose from around 19 million in 1939 to over 30 million in 1945.

SOURCE K

A scene from the popular wartime film, Millions Like Us

SOURCE L

The British public must be convinced of German brutality. We should emphasize wherever possible the wickedness and evil perpetrated in the occupied countries.

Kenneth Clark, head of the Films Division of the Ministry of Information, writing in a policy document (1940)

TASKS

1. Explain three reasons why the cinema was important during the Second World War.

2. How useful is Source L to an historian studying the use of cinema during the Second World War?

3. Find out more about one of the popular films mentioned above. Explain the plot and why this film would have been approved of during the war.

THE IMPACT OF THE RADIO

The establishment and development of the radio

Another form of entertainment that had a big impact on people's lives in the first half of the twentieth century was the radio.

The first radios began to appear in people's homes in the 1920s. They were known as 'wireless' sets. A good valve set was expensive to buy for most people, but within a few years mass production of radios had brought the cost down to a level most people could afford. A new era was dawning, bringing information and entertainment to people in their own homes.

The government was reluctant to allow the spread of radio transmission, fearing it would interfere with the armed forces, but there was enough public demand to make it think again. The British Broadcasting Company was set up by the government in 1922. It was paid for by issuing radio licences rather than relying on commercial advertising as in the USA. In 1927, it was renamed the British Broadcasting Corporation and became a public company, which it remains today.

SOURCE A

An early radio licence issued in 1935

The BBC had two networks and offered a wide range of entertainment and information including dramas, classical music and news. Sport also began to feature in the schedules. The first FA Cup Final broadcast was Cardiff City's victory over Arsenal in 1927. Football commentators used a numbered code to tell radio listeners on which part of the pitch the action was taking place. Other sporting events attracted huge listening audiences, such as Welshman Tommy Farr's world heavyweight boxing bout with Joe Louis in 1937. The BBC's national service became a major source of entertainment for many people in Wales and England.

SOURCE B

I'm writing to say how much the wireless means to me and thousands of the same sort. It is our magic carpet. Before I got a week at Rhyl and that was all the travelling I did that wasn't on a tram. Now I can hear the Boat Race and the Derby and the chains being changed on the Menai Bridge. I can hear football on Saturday afternoons and talks by famous men and women who have travelled and can tell us about places.

A person from North Wales, writing in a letter published in the Radio Times Magazine in 1928

SOURCE C

Radio licences issued between 1923 and 1934

(Numbers of licences (millions) — Year)

- 1923: 200,000
- 1926: 1,800,000
- 1929: 2,600,000
- 1932: 4,300,000
- 1934: 5,700,000

Official figures showing numbers of radio licences, taken from BBC handbooks

The number of radio licences issued grew steadily through the 1920s and by 1935 half the households in Wales had radio licences. By this time, the BBC had begun to face competition from continental radio stations such as Radio Normandie and Radio Luxembourg.

Radio was there to record several historic moments for posterity. One such event was the declaration of war against Germany in 1939. This was the first time such a significant moment was conveyed to this nation by radio. Prime Minister Chamberlain told listeners "it is evil things we shall be fighting against."

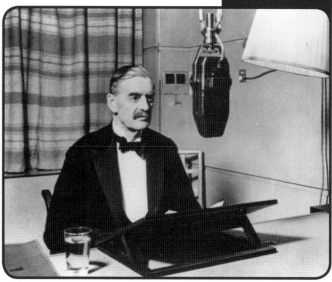

Neville Chamberlain, the British Prime Minister, announcing the declaration of war against Germany on the radio in 1939

The origins of television

Television was in its infancy between the wars. It was of little importance at this time. The Scottish engineer John Logie Baird was one of several pioneers of television, making the first regular experimental transmissions and broadcasting across the Atlantic in 1928.

The first BBC television broadcasts began in 1936, reaching a few thousand people living within 40-100 miles of the Alexandra Palace transmitter in London. A television with a dim 25 × 20 cm black and white screen could cost up to £100, the same price as a small car. Broadcasts, which included plays and newsreels, stopped in 1939 with the outbreak of war and did not restart until 1946.

TASKS

1. What does Source A show you about radio in the 1930s?

2. Use Source B and your own knowledge to explain why radio was a popular form of entertainment.

3. How useful is Source C in finding out about the popularity of radio in the 1930s?

4. Use an Internet site to listen to Chamberlain's speech in 1939. How do you think people would have felt listening to this radio broadcast?

5. Describe the early years of television.

Radio during the Second World War

As with the cinema, the government used radio to control news and information during the war. The Ministry of Information managed the radio, again recognising that radio also had a key role in keeping up people's morale.

Wireless was very important, we called it a wireless in those days not a radio. Our man at that time was Winston Churchill. Nobody ever missed one of Churchill's broadcasts. He gave people inspiration and he gave them encouragement. We would be in the park on a Sunday night and at about half-past eight there would be a mass exodus. People would be running home and looking at each other and saying, "Come on! You'll miss Churchill. He's on at nine o'clock." Everybody would be just scurrying out of the park and from then on they'd be crowded round the wireless.

Dougie Milburn, remembering his life during the Second World War in a local radio broadcast (2009)

The BBC started a new network in 1940 called *The Forces Programme*, which concentrated on variety shows, dance music and lecture talks. It was aimed at soldiers but was popular with civilians too. The BBC's Variety programme was moved to Bangor in North Wales in 1940 to avoid bombing. One of its most popular programmes was *ITMA (It's That Man Again)* with comedian Tommy Handley.

Stars of the radio show It's That Man Again *performing at a BBC studio in Bangor, 1942*

Reporting the news was very important. People relied on the radio for their news and broadcasts were carefully controlled. Military setbacks such as Dunkirk were made to sound less serious than they actually were, to keep up people's spirits. However, the BBC only broadcast stories it believed to be true as people were relying on their radio for up to date news.

The actual reading of the news carried a very great responsibility. It was up to us to instil a spirit of courage and hope into millions of listeners even in the very darkest days. There were times when the content of the bulletins made it very difficult. We would use carefully prepared language:

"Our troops have retired to carefully prepared positions"
"Fifteen of our aircrafts have gone off course"
"The Germans have reported some advance on the Russian front"
"Enemy aircraft were over this country last night and some damage and casualties have been reported"

Bruce Belfrage, a BBC newsreader during the war, quoted in the book, Reporting in the Twentieth Century *by Paul Terry (2002)*

TASKS

1. How useful is Source E to an historian studying the popularity of the radio during the Second World War?

2. What does Source F tell you about radio during the Second World War?

3. Look at Source G. It contains some selected language that newsreaders had to use. What do you think may have really happened in these incidents?

4. Find a website that has recordings of famous radio broadcasts from the Second World War. Listen to three radio broadcasts from the war. Evaluate them for their effectiveness.

5. Having studied both cinema and radio in this chapter, which do you think was the most important form of entertainment in the period up to 1945?

This section provides guidance on how to answer question 1(d) from Units 1 and 2. It involves the analysis and evaluation of the utility of a source and it is worth 6 marks.

Question 1(d) – the analysis and evaluation of the utility of a source

How useful is Source A to the historian studying the popularity of cinema in the 1930s?
[Explain your answer using the source and your own knowledge.]

[6 marks]

SOURCE A

And then at half past seven, all the lights would go out. But before they went out, there'd be a lot of fun. If there were boys sitting in the back row, and they fancied some of the girls, what do you think they'd pelt them with? Not roses. Monkey nuts! If you had monkey nuts thrown at you, at least you knew someone fancied you.

Hilda Richards, who was 15 at the time, remembering visits to a cinema in Milford Haven in 1934. Mrs Richards was interviewed by a school history group in 1992.

Tips on how to answer

This question will usually involve the analysis and evaluation of a primary source.

- In your answer you will need to **evaluate the usefulness** of this primary source in terms of its content, its origin and its purpose. Some schools find it useful to use memory aids to help structure answers. One of these involves looking at three aspects of the source in question:

CONTENT	ORIGIN	PURPOSE
What does the source say?	Who said it? When did they say it?	Why was it said? Who was it said to and why? Is it biased?

- You should aim to write about **two to three sentences** about the content of the source, putting the information into your own words and supporting it with your own knowledge of this topic.

- You should then **comment upon the author** of the source, noting when the source was written and under what circumstances.

- You should consider **why** the source was written and whether this makes the source **biased**. Remember that a biased source can still be very useful to the historian and do not just dismiss it.

- To obtain maximum marks your answer must contain **reasoned comments** upon each of the three elements. If you only write about the content of the source do not expect to get more than half marks.

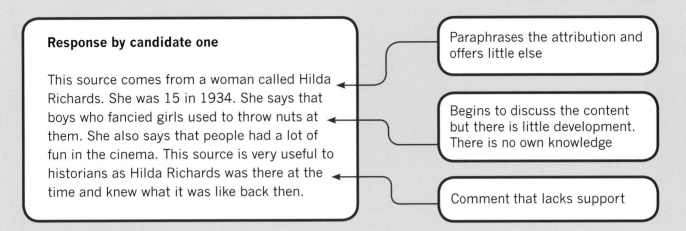

Response by candidate one

This source comes from a woman called Hilda Richards. She was 15 in 1934. She says that boys who fancied girls used to throw nuts at them. She also says that people had a lot of fun in the cinema. This source is very useful to historians as Hilda Richards was there at the time and knew what it was like back then.

Paraphrases the attribution and offers little else

Begins to discuss the content but there is little development. There is no own knowledge

Comment that lacks support

Response by candidate two

Source A is very useful to an historian because it is a memory from a lady who experienced the cinema at first hand in the 1930s. The source appears to be typical of the experience of many young people at this time. Mrs Richards remembers the fun element of a visit to the cinema, important especially as this is at the height of the Depression in south Wales.

She also proves that an important reason why many younger people went to the cinema at this time was not to marvel at the new technology of the talkies, but to date and to get dates.

She made these comments in 1992 to members of a school history group who may have been studying life during the Depression. It is highly likely that her comments are accurate as they confirm several well-known arguments about the popularity of the cinema at this time. Social historians would find her memories useful and humorous but would also realise that her experience may be unique to her or to her friends in her town. Other people will have had different reasons for the popularity of the cinema.

Refers to the author and supplies some context

Resists temptation to paraphrase content, but uses it to demonstrate wider knowledge of the topic area

Refers to the purpose of the source and questions its utility as an individual piece of memory

This candidate demonstrates a very high degree of understanding and is able to evaluate well. The content of the source is clearly understood and is used to place the source in the context of the period. Reference is made to the Depression and entertainment at this time. The author is identified, as is the issue of a memory of an individual, which would not impact on its usefulness, but which may need to be considered alongside other views.

The answer provided a full evaluation and will get the top level: 6 out of 6 marks.

Now you have a go

> Every day the BBC radio offered a variety of programmes – drama, sport, light and classical music, news, religion, talks, interviews, debates, comedy. This meant that as many tastes as possible could be satisfied and from time to time, various sections of the audience could be explicitly targeted: women, children, business people, farmers, soldiers and so on.

Andrew Crisell, an author and history lecturer, writing in a history book, An Introductory History of British Broadcasting *(1997)*

Question

How useful is this source to an historian studying the appeal of BBC radio in the 1930s?
[Explain your answer using the source and your own knowledge.]

[6 marks]

CHAPTER 5

WHAT WERE THE MAJOR DEVELOPMENTS THAT AFFECTED POPULAR ENTERTAINMENT IN WALES AND ENGLAND IN THE 1950s AND 1960s?

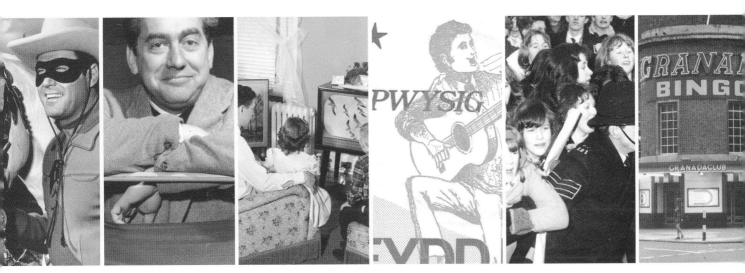

The decades after the period of austerity that followed the Second World War saw great changes in the ways in which people were entertained. Two forms of entertainment, which remain hugely influential today, made great strides in these decades – television and pop music. Cinema going remained high but faced real competition from television. Radio listening remained strong and radio was able to take advantage of new technology to re-invent itself in the 1960s. As in many aspects of life, it was the developments in the 1950s and 1960s that were to have a major influence on popular entertainment up to the present day.

TELEVISION

The growth of television in the 1950s

In 1946 there were 15,000 combined radio and television licences in Britain. Television availability was steadily extending across Britain, reaching most parts of Wales, the west of England and Scotland by the early 1950s. In South Wales the first BBC transmitting station opened in the village of Wenvoe in 1952. The first Welsh language television programme was broadcast

the same year. At this time the only television channel available was the BBC. For many, getting a television was still an expensive business and for most people in the early 1950s their experience of watching television was often in a friend's or neighbour's home.

Most historians agree that the coronation of Queen Elizabeth II in 1953 was the point when television began to replace radio as the main method of entertainment and communication in Britain. Over half the population watched the event.

SOURCE A

Martin was fiddling about with the television switches. Then the programme began and Anne gasped to see a man's face suddenly appear on the lighted screen of the set. "I can hear him *and* see him," she whispered to Julian. Mr Curton heard her and laughed. "But your dog can't smell him or he'd be after him!" It was great fun seeing the television programme.

Extract from the children's adventure book, Five on Kirrin Island Again, *by Enid Blyton (1947)*

SOURCE B

The Coronation was due on June 2nd so Dad went and rented a TV set. We were suddenly the most popular people in the street. We only had a small bungalow and the set was in the little dining room. The table went in the corner and the chairs were spread around. Some people brought their own. Friends, neighbours and even the vicar squeezed in and they all brought food for lunch.

Mrs P Gerrish, who answered a radio appeal for memories of growing up in the 1950s (1990)

SOURCE C

A family watching television in the 1950s. The parents are watching television with the children. The father has monopolised the chair while his wife and children perch on the arm or sit on stools

Commercial television

In 1955, the government decided to allow the introduction of **commercial television**, which broke the monopoly of the BBC. Commercial television was to be funded mainly by advertisements. Independent television, which became known as ITV, was set up with separate regional companies who had to compete to win the franchise to broadcast in their region. The first ITV broadcasts were in London, the Midlands and the south of England. The first advert seen on British television was for Gibbs SR toothpaste.

Wales got its own commercial television in 1958 run by TWW (Television Wales and the West) followed by WWN (Wales West and North / Teledu Cymru) in 1962. TWW took over WWN in 1963 before losing the franchise to HTV in 1968.

At first people had to buy a special adaptor to receive ITV. The independent companies lost money to start with because of the high costs of start-up and programme making. ITV bosses were also worried that their programmes would not be popular enough with the public, many of whom were used to BBC programming.

Because of this, many early ITV channels were similar to the BBC station only with adverts. However attitudes soon changed, as Source D shows. ITV grew quickly in popularity and in 1958 it claimed to have 79% of viewers who had a choice of the two channels. In 1957 Roy Thomson, the controller of Scottish TV, described commercial television as 'a licence to print your own money.'

SOURCE D

Let's face it – once and for all. The public likes girls, wrestling, bright musicals, quiz shows and real-life drama. We gave them the Halle Orchestra, Foreign Press Club and visits to the local fire station. Well we've learnt. From now on, what the public wants, the public gets.

A programme controller for Associated Rediffusion, which ran the ITV channel for London, explaining a change in company policy (1959)

Well, you could say that it [ITV] wasn't approved of in our house. I just thought it was a dreadful waste of time and I didn't like it. There was too much cheap entertainment and not really enough education. I didn't want the boys to get used to watching it so I used to ban it.

A woman from Leicestershire, remembering her early reaction to commercial television in the late 1950s

TASKS

1. How useful is Source A to an historian studying television in the 1950s?

2. Use Source B and your own knowledge to explain why many people wanted to buy television sets in the 1950s.

3. What does Source C show you about family life in the 1950s?

4. Describe the growth of commercial television in the 1950s.

5. Look at Sources D and E. Why do these people have different views about commercial television?

THE DEVELOPMENT AND IMPACT OF TELEVISION

SOURCE A

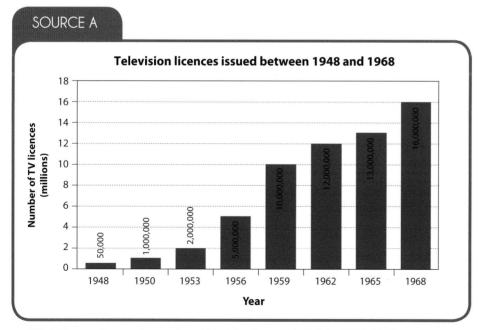

Television licences issued between 1948 and 1968

Official figures showing the number of television licences in Britain, 1948-1968

By 1966 85% of homes had a television. In that year the average price of a television set was about £70 and the average wage was around £12 per week. A television still remained quite an expensive purchase. Most people either bought their televisions on hire purchase or rented them from hire companies who had showrooms on every high street. At this time, television programmes were still shown in black and white. Colour television was first shown on BBC2 in 1967.

Television landmarks in the 1960s

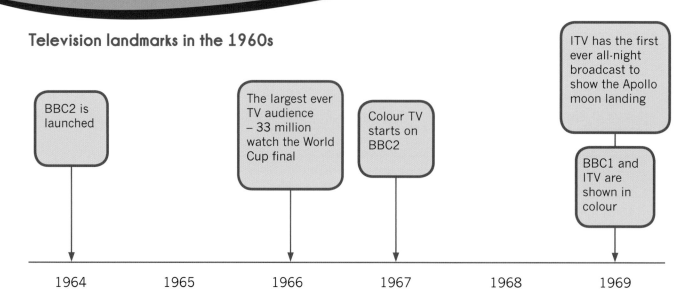

During the 1960s in particular, the impact of television on people's lives grew enormously. An increasing range of programmes was produced to cater for everyone's tastes. Many of these were very influential and helped shape the future of television programming:

- **Situation comedies** such as *Steptoe and Son* and *Hancock's Half Hour* (this was a huge radio hit in the 1950s and was successfully turned into a TV show);
- **Police dramas** such as *Dixon of Dock Green* and *Z Cars*;
- **Satire** such as *That Was The Week That Was* and *Monty Python's Flying Circus*;
- **Science fiction** such as *Doctor Who* and *Stingray* (a cartoon show, which was the first ITV programme to be filmed in colour);
- **Sport** such as *Grandstand* and *World of Sport*;

- **Soap operas** such as *Coronation Street* and *Emergency Ward 10* (these were based on an idea already established on radio shows such as *The Archers*);
- **Children's shows** such as *Blue Peter* and *Crackerjack*;
- **Pop music** shows such as *Juke Box Jury* and *Disc a Dawn*;
- **News programmes**, which brought key events such as the Cuban Missile Crisis and the Apollo moon landing into people's homes.

SOURCE B

Television programmes on Saturday 12th September 1964			
BBC		**TWW (ITV)**	
1pm	Grandstand		
5.15	The Tele Goons	5.15	Lassie
5.30	Dr Who	5.45	The News
5.55	Juke Box Jury	5.50	Lucky Stars Summer Spin
6.20	The News		
6.30	Hob y Deri Dando	6.35	Sugarfoot
6.55	Rugby Special		
7.20	Dr Finlay's Casebook	7.25	Opportunity Knocks
8.10	Club Variety Night	8.10	Film
8.55	Perry Mason	9.20	The News
9.45	Diary of a Young Man	9.35	Sergeant Cork – Victorian Detective
10.30	The News		
10.45	The Third Man	11.05	Crusade in Europe
11.10	Weather	12am	Close
11.15	Close		

The front cover of the Radio Times *magazine, 1964*

Tony Hancock, one of the most popular radio and television stars of the 1950s and early 1960s

SOURCE E

I think the television must have been the biggest change in the lives of children this century. Before that, children spent so much more of their time out playing and exploring, especially in the summer. But television changed our lives – it gave us entertainment at the flick of a switch. I also think it meant we discovered less for ourselves than our parents did.

Gill McAleer, born in 1954, interviewed for a BBC TV documentary on childhood in the twentieth century

TASKS

1. How useful is Source A to an historian studying entertainment in the 1950s and 1960s?

2. Find out more about the important landmarks on the timeline. Which of these do you think was the most significant in the history of television?

3. Investigate one of the television shows mentioned. Explain why it was popular and why it has influenced the development of television programmes.

4. Look at Source B. The subject of some of these programmes is clear, but others not so clear. Try to find out what these programmes were about. How many of these types of programmes are still shown today?

5. How far does Source E support the view that television was the biggest change in entertainment in the twentieth century?

CINEMA

Cinema – one of the key forms of entertainment in the 1930s and the war years – continued to be very popular in the 1950s. However, by the 1960s it was greatly affected by the growing development of television as a form of mass entertainment.

Continuing popularity in the 1950s

In the 1950s, the Hollywood-produced feature films remained really popular. Stars who became household names included Marilyn Monroe, John Wayne, Humphrey Bogart and Lauren Bacall.

The cinema also remained a real source of entertainment for many children in the 1950s. Television was only just taking off, and would have to be watched with the rest of the family. At the cinema you were with your mates and the pictures were in 'glorious Technicolor'. Many children still visited the Saturday morning **matinées** in their local cinemas.

SOURCE C

The Lone Ranger, *a popular cinema (and later television) hero of the 1950s*

The decline in cinema attendance

From the late 1950s the popularity of cinema quickly declined. This was due to many reasons, including:

- A rise in ticket prices, as the government increased Entertainment Tax;
- There was little money and few materials available for repairing or rebuilding cinemas so they became scruffy and shabby;
- Television was on the rise. In 1945 there were only 15,000 television sets in Britain. In 1961 there were 11 million.

Many cinemas were forced to close down and were demolished. Others were converted for different uses: shops, nightclubs and discos or bingo halls. Abertillery used to have four cinemas, but only one was left by 1964. Some cinemas tried new gimmicks to keep their audience, such as Smell-o-vision and 3D but the novelty soon wore off. Blockbuster films such as the James Bond movies and films featuring pop groups like the Beatles continued to bring in the crowds on occasion. However, regular attendances plummeted as people stayed home.

SOURCE D

Who would want to go out to a cold, draughty cinema with décor that had not been painted or repaired since the 1930s and pay prices that had risen much faster than inflation, when television could entertain you more cheaply in the warmth of your own fireside every month?

Chris Culpin, a teacher and historian, writing in a school textbook, Making History *(1996)*

SOURCE E

The telly made all these things seem twenty times bigger than we'd ever thought they were. Even adverts at the cinema were tame because we were now seeing them in private at home. We used to cock our noses up at things in shops that didn't move but suddenly we saw their real value because they jumped and glittered around the screen and had some [woman] going head over heels to get her nail-polished grabbers on them.

A character in the novel Saturday Night and Sunday Morning, *written by Alan Sillitoe (1958)*

SOURCE F

The Granada in Lambeth in 1963. This large cinema opened in 1932. By 1955, seat capacity was down and by 1961 the cinema had closed. By 1962, the building was running as Granada Bingo with wrestling on Saturdays and bingo every night

SOURCE G

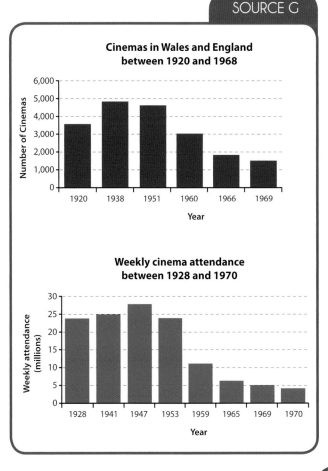

1. Explain why cinema was popular with young audiences in the 1950s.

2. Explain why fewer people went to the cinema by the 1960s.

3. How far does Source D support the view that television was responsible for the decline of cinema?

4. Use Source F and your own knowledge to explain what happened to many cinemas in Wales and England in the 1960s.

5. Find out what had happened to the cinemas in your area by the 1960s.

THE INCREASING IMPACT OF POPULAR MUSIC

Up until the 1950s, although **record players** were a common sight in homes, most people who wanted to listen to music were more likely to turn on the radio than put on a record. Records broke and scratched easily and radio was cheaper. From the 1950s however, more and more people starting buying records. Young people in particular bought singles to play at home or put money into **jukeboxes** in coffee bars and pubs.

Over the next 50 years, popular music became a central part of many people's lives. For many young people it can be argued that the influence of popular music was as great as that of television.

The development of musical styles

The 1950s: rock'n'roll

After the Second World War crooners like Frank Sinatra and Bing Crosby, and big bands inspired by the late US bandleader Glenn Miller, dominated popular music. These could be listened to on the radios found in every home, but increasingly people would enjoy live shows. In 1951 there were 450 dance halls such as the Mecca and Locarno chains, as well as thousands of other smaller halls and ballrooms. These were mostly for adults rather than teenagers and featured dancing to live big bands and their singers.

In the mid 1950s a new kind of popular music arrived from America. **Rock'n'roll** was based on black rhythm and blues but mainly performed by white artists. British youth was excited by the energetic music of Billy Haley and Elvis Presley that was built on the basic structure of guitar, bass and drums with occasional piano. This was music for young people, not their parents. Many commentators felt that this new music was a passing phase. They were to be quite wrong in their prediction.

By the end of the 1950s there were at least 300 rock'n'roll groups in Liverpool alone. Britain even developed its own musical style, **skiffle**, inspired by the records of Lonnie Donegan. Older people thought that the simple, homemade skiffle groups were more wholesome than the raucous rock'n'roll style.

SOURCE A

For anyone who grew up during the 1950s, or anyone familiar with the music of the time, the term "skiffle" can bring a nostalgic sigh. Long before punk, it was the first DIY music: master three chords on the guitar, find a book of American folk songs and you could do it. It was, to all intents and purposes, the first British rock music, before electric guitars and drum kits began to dominate. In hindsight there seems to be an innocence about it, but at the time it was the sound of full-blooded teenage rebellion.

From a website dedicated to the history of pop music (2009)

SOURCE B

A new singer from America is a raw young southerner, Mr Elvis Presley, only twenty-one, who combines a hillbilly style of wailing with bodily contortions. His records, such as *Heartbreak Hotel* and *Hound Dog*, have sold something in the region of 10 million copies, and whatever his appeal, Mr Presley has become a national craze.

From an article in The Times *newspaper (September 1956)*

If you appreciate good singing, I don't suppose you'll manage to hear this disc all the way through.

A critic reviewing the Elvis Presley record, Heartbreak Hotel, *in the* New Musical Express *magazine (February 1956)*

Bill Haley and his Comets had performed in Cardiff in 1957. They were condemned by the city authorities who were appalled to hear that the audience had danced in the aisles. In Wales, there was the popular *Parti Sgiffl Llandygai*, which astounded those who believed that Welsh music stopped with hymns and playing the harp.

John Davies, an historian, writing in a history book, A History of Wales *(1990)*

The 1960s: the Swinging Sixties

The popular performers of the 1950s dominated the early 1960s. Soon however, one British group was about to change the whole face of pop music.

The Beatles, from Liverpool, had embraced the new rock'n'roll style and developed an exciting new sound based on harmony singing, two guitars and a powerful bass guitar and drum section. They were also confident and bright working class youths with real song writing talent and cheeky humour. After their first single, *Love Me Do* got to number 17 in the charts in 1962, they went on to have an incredible run of chart success, both in Britain and in the USA; they were the first British group to make it in America.

The Beatles influenced thousands of similar groups, and other British groups became highly successful and influential in their own right; these included the Rolling Stones, the Hollies, the Who and the Kinks. These bands had a huge impact on the lives of young fans all over the world.

Every part of Britain seemed to have its own local stars. In Swansea, it was the Jets and the Bystanders; the valleys of South Wales had the Human Beans and Tommy Scott and the Senators (Tommy Scott later changed his name to Tom Jones). Later in the decade, the Sain record label was founded in Cardiff by Dafydd Iwan and Huw Jones and provided a launch pad for many Welsh language acts. It was to become Wales' leading record company.

Police hold back Beatles fans as the group arrive at a hotel in London in 1964

The atmosphere was electric as soon as we got in the door. When the Beatles came on the place went up in a sound I could not have imagined with girls screaming – we could just about hear the music! The Beatles were really funny and the music we could hear was fantastic. I soon joined in the screaming. Mum and especially Dad were somewhat bemused for quite some time afterwards but my sister and I came out with buzzing ears, hearts pounding and a sense of excitement never before experienced.

Jean Quinn, who was taken to a Beatles concert on Llandudno Pier by her parents in 1963. She remembered the occasion in an email to her son who was carrying out research on the 1960s

Older people weren't so impressed, especially after the Beatles were given MBEs in 1965 for their contribution to British exports.

Many other different musical styles developed during the decade. As well as the beat groups, there was Californian surf music highlighted by the Beach Boys. The soul of the Motown record label made stars of artists like the Supremes and Aretha Franklin. Bob Dylan and the Scottish artist Donovan led the folk movement. Later in the decade, there developed the psychedelic music of west coast American bands such as the Grateful Dead and Jefferson Airplane.

SOURCE G

There's no dignity left in it now. At one time I was proud of my OBE, but not any more. I believe that the time has come for a strong protest against these pop groups and I hope that by returning my medal I can make somebody take notice.

Captain David Evans, explaining to a journalist why he returned his OBE in protest at the honours awarded to the Beatles (1965)

SOURCE H

Teenagers spend most of their time listening to pop music and this medium of expression provides the best means for celebrating our 21st anniversary. This is something new for the church in Corris and I hope the older parishioners will not form an opinion before they have experienced the service.

Reverend Glyn Morgan of Holy Trinity Church, Corris, explaining why he invited the Xenons, a pop group from Aberystwyth to play at a special service in his church (September 1964)

TASKS

1. Why do you think the authors of Sources B and C had different views about Elvis Presley?

2. How far does Source E support the view that pop music could lead to trouble?

3. Look at Sources G and H. Why do they have different views about the influence of pop music?

4. Make up a play list of ten 1960s records for a disco for your school.

5. Choose a major pop music act from the 1950s or 1960s and explain their importance.

The impact of pop music in the 1960s

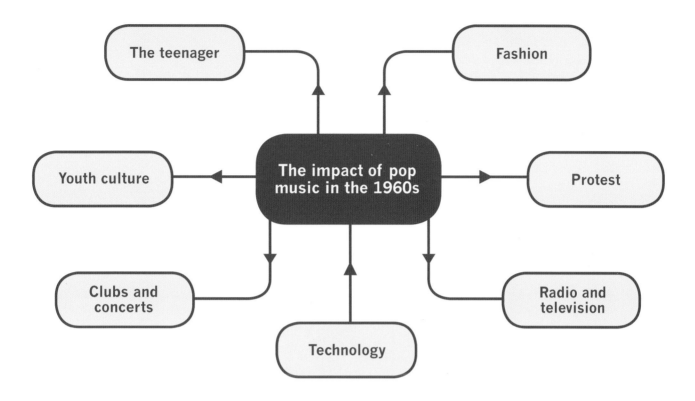

The impact of pop music in the 1960s

- The teenager
- Fashion
- Youth culture
- Protest
- Clubs and concerts
- Radio and television
- Technology

The evolution of the teenager

By 1964 there were 6 million teenagers in the UK who spent £1.5 billion a year. Pop music spawned lots of businesses to encourage them to spend their money. Over 100 million records were sold in 1964. Other merchandise on offer could range from magazines, lampshades, posters, drinks, badges, toys, lipsticks and even cans of 'Beatle-breath'. The media had started to write about a 'generation gap' between teenagers and their older relatives. Pop music had certainly helped to develop this.

SOURCE A

Posters advertising Beatles merchandise

SOURCE B

People try to put us d-down
Just because we get around
Things they do look awful c-cold
Hope I die before I get old

Opening lyrics from the song My Generation, *by the Who (1964)*

Fashion

Just like the movie stars of the 1930s, the pop stars of the 1960s were highly influential in changing fashion styles. Young people flocked to wear the same style of clothes as their idols, such as the leather jacket, the mini-skirt, the parka and flowered shirts. Hairstyles ranged from mop-tops to long hair and Afros for men and from beehives to pageboy cuts for women.

Typical 1960s fashion (1967)

Forget the mods and the rockers. Forget the lunatic fringe of unwashed pill-takers, scruffy beatniks and hairy layabouts. The truth is that they are outnumbered ten to one by the normal decent young people of Britain. They don't take drugs. They don't get drunk. But they do live tremendously exciting lives at a breathless pace that completely baffles their confused mothers and fathers. Whatever activity they engage in, from dancing until dawn to ten-pin bowling, they plunge into it with a tremendous and dynamic zest.

Arthur Helliwell, a journalist writing in the Sunday People *newspaper (September 1966)*

Youth culture

Young people in the 1960s didn't all dress and think the same. Separate youth cultures developed, each with their own styles of dress, behaviour and music. These included the Mods, the Rockers and later the hippies. The press enjoyed highlighting each group and their characteristics, including gang fights at the seaside and rampant drug taking and nudity at pop festivals. However these were the minority. Most young people just enjoyed their records and occasionally annoying their parents.

Protest

From its earliest years, rock'n'roll was seen as a form of rebellion. In the 1960s, pop music became more closely linked to political protest. American singers like Bob Dylan and Joan Baez protested against nuclear weapons and the Vietnam War. Sam Cooke wrote *A Change is Gonna Come*, which became an anthem of the Civil Rights movement in the USA and was resurrected in 2008 as a campaign song for Barrack Obama. Even though most protest singers were American, they had a tremendous influence on young people in Britain who were introduced to many political issues through protest songs. In Wales, singers like Dafydd Iwan and Huw Jones drew inspiration from political causes such as the Tryweryn reservoir controversy and the investiture of Prince Charles in the late 1960s.

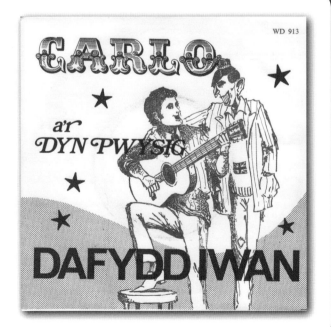

The cover of the single Carlo *by Welsh language singer Dafydd Iwan, released on the Sain record label in 1969. The song was a protest against the investiture of Prince Charles*

Clubs and concerts

There were giant rock festivals like the one at Woodstock in New York State, which attracted over 500,000 fans. In the UK there were huge open-air festivals in Hyde Park in London and on the Isle of Wight from 1968-1970. Elsewhere, many more people started going regularly to see live bands and singers in theatres and clubs. Towards the end of the decade, the discothéque had begun to get popular, where people danced and listened to recorded music played by disc jockeys.

This nomadic band of pop followers put up with extraordinary discomfort for the sake of their music. For a supposedly "undisciplined" generation they are remarkably orderly about queuing. They queue to get into the pub in the village, for the cold water taps and to go to the lavatories. In the field you stake your claim to a piece of floor simply by rolling out your sleeping bag and leaving it there. Nobody disturbs your claim. As the evening gets colder the compére jokes that two in a sleeping bag are probably warmer than one. This raises scarcely a murmur of laughter. Everybody knows that.

Dave Wilsworth, reporting for ITV news from the Isle of Wight festival (August 31st 1969)

The Dansette played a large part in the formation of the new generation of the 50s and 60s known as "the teenager". The bedroom was no longer just a place to sleep; it was the place where pop music established its place in most family homes. Downstairs was for parents to watch TV and upstairs was for playing records! For teenagers it was not just a necessity but also a way of life.

A tribute written to the record player called the Dansette, recorded on a website devoted to the memory of the device (2009)

Technology

Technology and pop music were perfect partners. In the 1950s the heavy, fragile 78 rpm singles had been replaced by lighter '45s'. In the 1960s, groups began to develop their ideas on long-playing albums (LPs). Companies developed electric record players to replace the wind-up gramophones. In this period, transistor radios were developed. These were light, cheap and could run off batteries. They were a perfect invention for listening to pop music. People could take their radio to work, around the house, to the beach or in the car.

The media

Unlike cinema, radio was far from dying in the 1950s and 1960s. It showed its versatility by adapting to changing tastes and finding new audiences. The BBC had launched new channels in the 1950s, including the Light Programme for more entertaining features and the Third Programme for more serious material. However, the growing popularity of pop music was to lead to a greater change. There was a demand for a radio station dedicated to pop music. This need was fulfilled by channels broadcasting from Europe and also by the pirate radio stations that avoided the law on radio frequencies by broadcasting from ships off the English coast. The best known of these was Radio Caroline. In 1967 the government bowed to pressure from listeners and allowed the BBC to set up a pop music channel, Radio 1.

A publicity photograph of Tony Blackburn, the first breakfast time DJ on Radio 1 in 1967

Television had already reacted to the influence of pop music. ITV made a star of Cathy McGowan who presented *Ready Steady Go* and in 1964 the BBC had responded by setting up the long-running *Top of the Pops*, which showcased hit records and groups in the charts.

Music papers and magazines like *Melody Maker*, *Sounds* and *New Musical Express* also influenced and reflected the musical and fashion tastes of young people.

SOURCE I

Cathy was an early patron of Biba. All the girls aped Cathy's long hair and eye-covering fringe and soon their little faces were growing heavy with stage make-up, just like their idol.

Barbara Hulanicki, the founder of influential 1960s fashion store Biba, recalling the influence that pop presenter Cathy McGowan had on young girls in the mid 1960s

TASKS

1. Use Sources A and B to explain how teenagers were influenced by pop music.

2. Look at Source D. How far does this source support the view that all young people were troublemakers in the 1960s?

3. Use clips from a website to look at 5 famous protest songs. Which one do you think is most effective?

4. Read Source F. Why would young people put up with such bad conditions at a pop festival?

5. Use Source G and your own knowledge to explain how pop music influenced technology in the 1950s and 1960s.

6. Having studied both television and popular music in this chapter, which do you think was the more influential form of entertainment in the 1950s and 1960s? Explain your answer.

This section provides guidance on how to answer question 1(e) from Units 1 and 2. The question deals with historical interpretation through the analysis, evaluation and cross-referencing of two sources.

Question 1(e) – explain differences in interpretations

Why do Sources A and B have different views about youth culture in the 1960s?
[In your answer you should refer to both the content of the sources and the authors.]

[8 marks]

These sources say different things about the trouble associated with youth culture in the 1960s.
They relate to an incident in Clacton in 1964.

SOURCE A

Front page of the Daily Mirror, *March 1964*

SOURCE B

The papers built up a whole series of myths about the Clacton weekend. The papers spoke of 'gangs' – much too strong a word to describe the small groups of friends which had visited the seaside. They spoke as if all had come from London on their motorbikes or scooters, whereas most were not Londoners and had travelled by train and bus. They also stressed the damage and violence but the amount of either was about normal for the average Bank Holiday. Residents of Clacton were more annoyed by the noise made by the riders as they raced around the town.

Sociologist S. Cohen, writing in a history of the mods and rockers, Folk devils and moral panics: the creation of mods and rockers
(1972)

Tips on how to answer

You need to refer to the content of both sources, relate this to your own knowledge of this period and consider the attributions. This will require you to perform a thorough evaluation of both sources.

● You need to read through both sources with care, **underlining** or **highlighting** the most important details. You can also scribble some **notes in the margin** around the source about how it fits into your knowledge of this period:
  • Does it confirm what you know?
  • Does it only refer to part of the answer and are some important points missing?
  • Does it agree or disagree with what is said in the other source?
● This will enable you to **compare and contrast** the two sources in terms of their content value.
● You now need to consider the **origin** of each source, saying who the authors are and when they made these observations.
  E.g. Which one is the interpretation?

- You should then consider the **purpose** of each source, noting the **circumstances** under which they were written.

  E.g. Is the source written by a modern historian or a contemporary? Does the author display a biased point of view and if so, why?
- To obtain maximum marks you need to produce a **balanced answer** with **good support** from both sources and your own knowledge, together with a **detailed consideration of the attributions** of each source.

Response by candidate one

Source A is from the Daily Mirror. It says wild ones invade seaside 97 arrests. It doesn't like youth culture in the 1960s because it caused trouble at the seaside and spoiled people's holidays from their hard days spent at work. Source B is written by S Cohen who is a historian who is writing about mods and rockers. These were the people who started the trouble by the seaside. S Cohen says that there were gangs and motorbikes but not as much as people thought. He says that residents of Clacton were more annoyed by the noise made by the riders as they raced around the town.

Copies or paraphrases material from both sources

Slight hint at own knowledge

No real attempt to answer the question set

Examiner's comment

This is a weak answer. The candidate makes no clear attempt to address the set question about why there may be a difference in the views shown about youth culture. The candidate relies mostly on copying or paraphrasing the sources presented. Usually this would be a level 1 answer, but there are hints of some wider understanding, especially in the second sentence.

The answer reaches level 2 and gains 3 marks.

Response by candidate two

The sources give very different views of the trouble caused by youth culture in the 1960s. The Bank Holiday Monday in 1964 had seen a series of disturbances in seaside resorts between two groups of teenagers – the Mods and the Rockers.

Source A is the front page of the Daily Mirror newspaper that was published at Easter 1964. The headline of the paper is saying that there were 97 people arrested and that they were 'wild ones' who were behaving like animals. There is also a picture of a group of young people being arrested by a policeman with a large savage looking dog. I would expect newspapers like the Daily Mirror to be accurate and to tell the news truthfully. They would have had a reporter at the scene and they definitely had a photographer to record the incident. However, newspaper front pages are often inaccurate and can exaggerate things because they sell more papers to the public.

Source B has a different viewpoint from Source A. It comes

Considers the content and standpoint expressed in Source A from a book about mods and rockers. These were the groups who were supposed to be fighting in Clacton in 1964. Source B says that the trouble in Clacton was not as bad as the newspapers made it out to be. The author, S. Cohen, is an historian who would have researched this topic well and the information is likely to be balanced and informed. He would have had time to consult a range of evidence and therefore produce a balanced account. Because this book was published in 1972, he is likely to have been able to talk to people who were connected with the events, mods and rockers and people living in Clacton. Source B tells a very different story to that provided in Source A.

The two sources say opposite things about the trouble caused by youth culture because of the audiences for which they were produced. Source A is produced to create an effect on the readers. It is an example of a newspaper building up things to make them seem more important. Source B was written by a person who is obviously interested in the subject and I think his view is more likely to be the right one.

> Considers the content and standpoint expressed in Source B

> Compares the two sources and offers an explanation for the differences. Offers a judgement, although not really required

Examiner's comment

This is a well-developed answer. The candidate has performed a thorough evaluation of each source, with clear reference to differences in content and circumstances under which each was produced. The content has been explained and put into context, linking the material to the bigger picture. There is a good consideration of both attributions, spelling out the reasons for any reliability issues. The concluding paragraph compares and contrasts both sources and does offer a judgement, which is welcomed, if not strictly required.

The answer reaches the highest level and is worthy of receiving the maximum 8 marks.

Now you have a go

Why do Sources C and D have different views about pop groups in the 1960s?
[In your answer you should refer to both the content of the sources and the authors.]   [8 marks]

SOURCE C

The atmosphere was electric as soon as we got in the door. When the Beatles came on the place went up in a sound I could not have imagined with girls screaming – we could just about hear the music! The Beatles were really funny and the music we could hear was fantastic. I soon joined in the screaming. Mum and especially Dad were somewhat bemused for quite some time afterwards but my sister and I came out with buzzing ears, hearts pounding and a sense of excitement never before experienced.

Jean Quinn, remembering a Beatles concert on Llandudno Pier in 1963. She was interviewed for a research project into the 1960s (2009)

SOURCE D

There's no dignity left in it now. At one time I was proud of my OBE, but not any more. I believe that the time has come for a strong protest against these pop groups and I hope that by returning my medal I can make somebody take notice.

Captain David Evans, explaining to a journalist why he returned his OBE in protest at the honours awarded to the Beatles (1965)

CHAPTER 6

HOW HAS MASS ENTERTAINMENT IN WALES AND ENGLAND DEVELOPED IN RECENT TIMES?

THE CONTINUED APPEAL OF POP MUSIC

Pop music continued to have a great influence on entertainment after the 1960s. To some extent the years since then are too recent for historians to have a clear picture of the real impact. However, there is no doubt that pop music has had a huge impact on lifestyles, the media and technology. Many different musical styles and devices have come and gone but all have left an effect on people's lifestyles.

Varieties of pop music – 1970s

The 1970s were famous for **glam rock** artists like David Bowie, Marc Bolan, Elton John and the Sweet. They wore make-up and outrageous costumes to play loud electric pop music. The 1970s also saw the creation of the **'teenybopper'**, young music fans that were fanatical followers of David Cassidy, Donny Osmond or the Bay City Rollers. As in the 1960s, the music business was ready to supply the teenyboppers with all the merchandise needed.

The pop music sounds of the 1970s were challenged towards the end of the decade by the emergence of

SOURCE A

It was awful being injured and carried out on a stretcher, but apart from that it was really fantastic. I had never seen the Rollers on stage before, although I'd been a fan since they started. I'd go through it all again, if my parents would let me.

Lesley Jones, interviewed in the Daily Mirror *newspaper after being injured at a Bay City Rollers concert in May 1975*

punk rock. Punk groups set out to shock people and they were arguably the most controversial style of the late twentieth century. Groups like the Clash, the Damned and the Sex Pistols were fast, loud and brash – energy was more important than knowing how to play an instrument. The image of the pop star as 'the boy next door' was gone. Like many other trends inspired by pop music, the real influence of punk was limited. Most teenagers gazed in awe at the fashions from a distance but never got involved. However, the media treated the punks as a symptom of a broken society just like they had the Mods and Rockers in Clacton 12 years earlier. This reaction became stronger especially after the Sex Pistols used swear words on live television. Later in the month the punk group played a concert at Caerphilly and local Christians staged a protest vigil outside the hall.

The national media were going nuts suggesting the Sex Pistols were the devil's spawn and that the world was coming to an end. I was shocked at the ferocity and the intolerance of the reaction. I went to Caerphilly expecting a small demonstration, but there was 150 plus there and police all over the place. I thought the whole thing was less about the Sex Pistols and more of a comment on British society and media at the time.

Wayne Nowaczyk, a reporter on the local Rhymney Valley Express, *interviewed for a BBC TV documentary. He was sent to report on the Sex Pistols' concert in Caerphilly on December 14th 1976*

Front page of the Daily Mirror *newspaper on December 2nd 1976, after the Sex Pistols appearance on the Today programme*

I was conducting the hymns and when I look back now and see the couple of young people creeping in there I feel absolutely ashamed of myself. I've got great regrets when I look back at it because who am I, a fuddy-duddy councillor, to tell young people what they should listen to, what they should enjoy and how they should conduct themselves and their lives? We should try and put a plaque there to the Sex Pistols to commemorate the event that took place in Caerphilly and I would be prepared to unveil it.

Ray Davies, a local councillor and one of the leaders who organized opposition to the gig after being approached by concerned mothers. He was interviewed for his views by the Western Mail *newspaper in 2006*

Varieties of pop music – 1980s and 1990s

By the 1980s, pop music was very big business. Huge amounts of money were spent on marketing groups like U2 and singers like Michael Jackson. Synthesisers, drum machines and computerised keyboards dominated pop music, with groups like the Human League and Duran Duran becoming very popular. Into the 1990s **'Britpop'** groups like Oasis and Blur looked back to the British bands of the mid 1960s for inspiration and the American grunge movement was spearheaded by the American band Nirvana. By the turn of the century, Welsh pop bands had become extremely successful, leading the media to talk about **'Cool Cymru'**. The best-known bands included Stereophonics, The Manic Street Preachers, Catatonia and the Super Furry Animals.

Word Gets Around is an excellent debut album. It opens with 'A Thousand Trees', which allows the confident Kelly Jones to immediately stamp his vocal authority on the album. Voice and guitar are evenly matched in tone, both gritty and dirty. And what about the fabulous melody in 'Local Boy in the Photograph'? Marvellous stuff!

Colin Larkin, a music critic, reviewing Stereophonics' first album in the guide All time top 1000 albums

Women in pop

Women pop stars were nothing new. In the 1960s and 1970s, singers like Cilla Black, Dusty Springfield, Mary Hopkins and Sandie Shaw were highly successful. Until the punk movement of the late 1970s it was rare to see women playing instruments or leading bands. Punk groups like the Slits and Siouxsie and the Banshees began to change this image. Many female artists of the 1980s and 1990s had a stronger, more independent image than their predecessors in the 1960s and 1970s. Madonna was one of the best selling acts of the 1980s and Tina Turner, a veteran of the 1960s, made a hugely successful comeback, while in Wales singer and songwriter Caryl Parry Jones fronted the popular band Bando. During the 1990s, singer Cerys Matthews brought Welsh pop music to the attention of the rest of the world and the Spice Girls cultivated a brash image with their slogan '**Girl Power**'. In the Brits Awards of 2009, there were more female acts nominated for awards than male acts.

Pop on television

Top of the Pops continued to entertain in the 1970s with glamorous dancers Pan's People eagerly watched by youngsters and their fathers. Late at night serious rock fans could watch 'Whispering' Bob Harris presenting the *Old Grey Whistle Test* on BBC2. The growth of satellite and cable television from the 1980s meant that there were more chances to broadcast music, with one channel – MTV – dedicated to showing pop videos. The rock video had by now become an essential part of marketing a record. Sales often depended on the quality of the video.

In the twenty-first century, one of the most obvious shifts created by pop music has been the tremendous popularity of television shows like *Pop Stars*, *Pop Idol* and *The X Factor* – singing competitions featuring aspiring singers drawn from public auditions. These are the natural successors of earlier **talent shows** such as *Opportunity Knocks* and *New Faces*. The combination of regular weekly shows, viewer voting and major publicity has meant that audience interest has been huge. However, shows like *The X Factor* have caused some controversy, as shown in Sources G and H.

Spice Girls dolls on sale, part of the massive music industry (1997)

The X Factor has put music back decades. It is a preposterous show and you have judges who have no recognisable talent apart from self-promotion, advising singers what to wear and how to look. It is appalling. The real shop floor for musical talent is pubs and clubs, that is where the original work is. But they are being closed down on a daily basis. The music industry has been hugely important to bringing in billions of pounds to the economy. If anyone thinks *The X Factor* is going to do that, they are wrong.

Sting, lead singer of the Police, commenting on The X Factor *in an interview in the* Evening Standard *newspaper, (November 2009)*

Sting reckons that *The X Factor* is nothing more than "televised karaoke", with the contestants having no other ability than to mimic well-established stars. The Police frontman also said: "The real shop floor for musical talent is pubs and clubs." Er, that's precisely why people like Jamie Archer are on the programme. He spent years performing in pubs and it got him absolutely nowhere. Now he plays to an audience of more than 16 million every week. The music industry has changed immeasurably since Sting dumped teaching to lecture us all on where we've gone wrong.

Fiona Phillips, a columnist in the Daily Mirror, *November 2009*

1. How useful is Source B to an historian studying the impact of punk rock in the 1970s?

2. How far does Source D back up the view that punk rock was a danger to society?

3. What does Source F tell you about the music industry in the 1990s?

4. Look at Sources G and H. Why do these people have different views about shows like *The X Factor*?

MUSIC AND TECHNOLOGY

Listening styles have changed hugely in the last 30 years. In the 1970s the transistor radio remained the norm in the home, but Sony introduced the **Walkman** in 1979, which let people listen to cassette tapes on their own with headphones. In the 1980s cassette sales overtook vinyl albums. **CD players** were first introduced in 1982 using digital laser technology to provide a better sound. By the 1990s CD sales had outstripped both cassettes and records. In the twenty-first century, the availability of digital music on the Internet meant that the listening device of choice became the **MP3 player**, the best known of which was the ipod. People could now listen to the music of their choice everywhere.

SOURCE A

In June 1979 the Walkman was announced to the public. The press laughed at it. Some claimed that nobody would be interested in a tape player without a record function. The company was unfazed by such criticism and pushed on with promotion. A month after the Walkman became available, it was sold out. In ten years Sony sold 50 million units. The term "Walkman" even entered our language, and it is listed as such in the Oxford English Dictionary.

Tom Hormby, a university professor, writing in an Internet article on the development of musical technology (2006)

SOURCE B

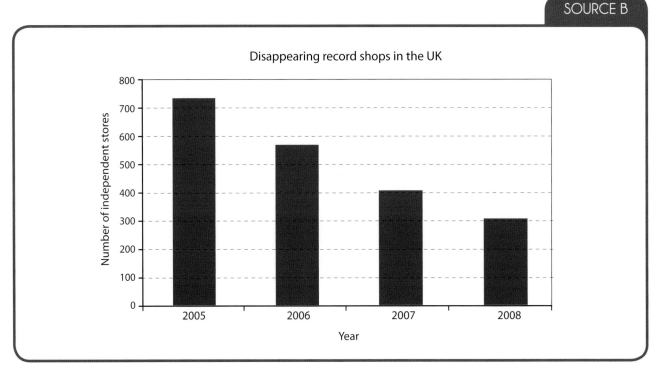

Disappearing record shops in the UK

Figures from the Entertainment Retailer's Association

Pop concerts and good causes

In the 1970s pop music was still involved with supporting worthy causes. Rock against Racism and CND both held big outdoor concerts in London to raise awareness of their causes. The 1980s saw the growth of large charity rock concerts. **Live Aid**, organized by Bob Geldof, raised millions for Ethiopian famine relief. Since then, many hundreds of records have been made to raise money for charity. It showed clearly how important and influential pop music had become in all areas of life.

SOURCE C

In 1985 my son Steven was born and was four months old when I watched the concert. I watched the footage as my son lay on the baby mat – he was healthy, happy, wanted, and loved. I watched the footage of many mothers losing their children daily. My heart went out to them. *Live Aid* reached me in a very deep and meaningful way. We had little money but I sent off a cheque for more than we could afford but a week without privileges was a small price to pay to support the cause.

Lorraine Haining, giving her memories of watching the Live Aid concert in 1985

SOURCE D

Pop music is incredibly effective. Pop performers are the priests of our time – they can draw attention to moral issues.

Larry Cox, director of Amnesty International, in a supportive message for a charity concert in 2006

SOURCE E

December 1984	Do They know it's Christmas	Band Aid	Famine in Ethiopia
June 1985	You'll never walk alone	The Crowd	Bradford City football disaster
April 1989	Ferry Across the Mersey	Gerry Marsden and friends	Hillsborough stadium disaster
September 1997	Candle in the Wind	Elton John	Princess Diana Memorial Fund
March 2005	Is this the way to Amarillo?	Tony Christie and Peter Kay	Comic Relief
July 2006	Don't stop me now	McFly	Sport Relief
November 2009	You Are not Alone	*X Factor* finalists	Great Ormond Street Appeal
February 2010	Everybody Hurts	20+ artists	Haiti earthquake appeal

Whether it is the range of musical styles, sounds, concerts, fashions or technology, there is no doubt that most people's lives have been greatly affected by the growth of popular music since the 1950s. There is no doubt that more change is on the way.

TASKS

1. Make up a timeline of how listening styles have changed since the 1970s.

2. How far does Source B support the view that ways of listening to music have changed in the twenty-first century?

3. Use Sources C and D and your own knowledge to explain why pop music is important to charity.

4. Make up a play list of 5 successful charity singles. Explain why you think these songs sold successfully.

5. 'Pop music has had a huge impact on entertainment since the 1980s.' How far do you agree with this statement? Explain your answer.

CHANGES IN TELEVISION AND CINEMA WATCHING

Television viewing

During the 1970s, the influence of television on people's lifestyles grew enormously with an increasing range of programmes to enjoy. The 1980s and 1990s were a time of increasing choice in television. In addition, the availability of video recorders and later, DVD recorders, meant that people were no longer tied to the hours of broadcast. There was also the introduction of breakfast-time TV and new channels. Channel 4, the second commercial channel, started in 1982 and aimed at providing programmes for minorities and groups with special interests. It also funded many new films and documentaries. Channel 5, the third commercial network, began in 1997 although not all areas were able to receive it.

The soap opera Brookside *made its debut on the first night of Channel 4 on 2 November 1982. The station actually bought thirteen existing houses in which to base the filming*

There are many people who watch ten or twelve hours of drama every week, sometime three or four hours a night, more in a month than even quite dedicated theatre-goers would have previously watched in a lifetime. This is drama of all sorts from classic plays to crime series to situation comedies. Most people in our society certainly spend more time watching television than they spend, for example, eating.

Raymond Williams, a novelist and critic, writing in an academic article, Technology and Society *(1979)*

Marge Simpson: "Bart, how many hours a day do you watch TV?"
Bart Simpson: "Six. Seven if there's something good on."

The Simpsons episode: When Flanders failed *(1994)*

Satellite and cable networks were first available in 1989 and offered a choice of news, sport, movies and repeats of popular terrestrial television shows, but for the first time viewers had to pay a subscription for these. Satellite and cable channels became increasingly popular after 2000 as the mushrooming of satellite dishes on many suburban streets shows. One of the biggest changes in television entertainment took place from 2008-2011 when the traditional analogue signal was gradually replaced by a digital signal, giving viewers even more choice of programmes.

A street in Newtown in 2002

Campaigning for Welsh language television

Before 1982 Welsh language television programmes were broadcast on BBC and ITV channels. *Cymdeithas yr Iaith Gymraeg* (the Welsh Language Society) campaigned for a separate Welsh language television channel; protesters were jailed for damaging broadcasting transmitters. The government was reluctant, but eventually changed its mind after Gwynfor Evans, the ex-leader of Plaid Cymru, threatened to go on hunger strike.

S4C – *Sianel Pedwar Cymru* – started broadcasting in 1982. The creation of S4C stimulated the television industry in Wales, funding new films and making Cardiff a world centre for animation. *Pobol y Cwm* became a daily soap opera in 1988, the longest running series in Europe after *Coronation Street* on ITV.

Superted, *one of the early successes for S4C, was first shown in November 1982*

The impact of TV

Since the 1950s, television has affected the lives of virtually everyone in Wales and England in some way. Some of the effects are generally accepted as being positive, while others are more controversial.

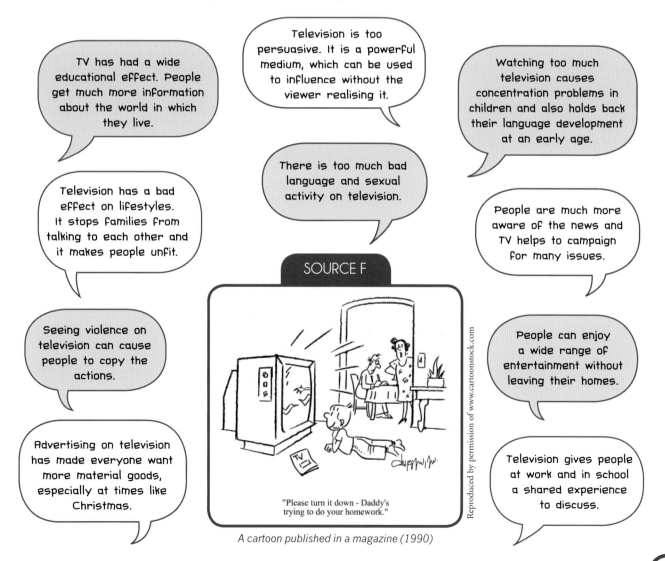

TV has had a wide educational effect. People get much more information about the world in which they live.

Television is too persuasive. It is a powerful medium, which can be used to influence without the viewer realising it.

Watching too much television causes concentration problems in children and also holds back their language development at an early age.

Television has a bad effect on lifestyles. It stops families from talking to each other and it makes people unfit.

There is too much bad language and sexual activity on television.

People are much more aware of the news and TV helps to campaign for many issues.

Seeing violence on television can cause people to copy the actions.

People can enjoy a wide range of entertainment without leaving their homes.

Advertising on television has made everyone want more material goods, especially at times like Christmas.

Television gives people at work and in school a shared experience to discuss.

SOURCE F

"Please turn it down - Daddy's trying to do your homework."

Reproduced by permission of www.cartoonstock.com

A cartoon published in a magazine (1990)

No technology before TV ever integrated faster into people's lives. Television took only 15 years to reach millions of households, while the telephone required 80 years; the car 50; and even radio needed 25. By 1983, moreover, the typical household was keeping the TV set turned on for more than five hours a day on average; two decades later this was up to eight hours a day and counting.

Gary R. Edgerton, a media historian, writing in a history book, The History of Television *(2007)*

Over the last 50 years TV has become the core of our culture. It used to be that children learned from three main sources: parents, teachers and religious leaders. These passed down the basic standards to live by. These three influences remain important but now they have a rival: television. And television has its own interests at heart. Television, for instance, has taught that the elderly and the poor are unimportant (few are ever shown); that there are far fewer female role models than male ones; and that almost everyone you want to be is well off, is white, and often lives in a house too expensive for average people to afford.

George Gerbner, a professor of media studies, speaking in a television documentary (2005)

TASKS

1. Choose either Source B or Source C. How far does this source support the view that people watch too much television?

2. How far does Source D support the view that satellite and cable channels were popular?

3. Explain why S4C was set up in 1982.

4. Use Source G and your own knowledge to explain how important television has been to people's lifestyles.

5. Does the author of Source H agree with the view expressed in Source G?

6. Work in groups. Create a balance sheet about whether you think the influence of television has been positive or negative. Support your opinion with evidence drawn from this chapter.

GOING TO THE CINEMA

Despite the film industry turning out thrillers, musicals, fantasies and dramas, cinema audiences continued to plummet in the 1970s and 1980s. Another blow was struck by the introduction of the video recorder in the 1980s so that people could now hire films to watch at home instead of going to the cinema. More and more cinemas began to close. Audiences declined to an all-time low of just 54 million visits a year in 1984 (about 1 million per week).

However, the film industry began to increase its share of entertainment in the 1990s. Special effects and high quality stereo sound meant that people wanted to see films like *Jurassic Park* and *Independence Day* on the big cinema screen, even if they hired or bought them on video later. Audiences began to increase for the first time since the Second World War. New, comfortable **multi-screen cinemas** were built and there were new developments in IMAX screens and 3D technology. Admissions recovered such that since 2000 they have remained above 150 million per year. They are unlikely to ever reach massive heights again though, as cinemas still have to compete with the home viewing experience.

SOURCE A

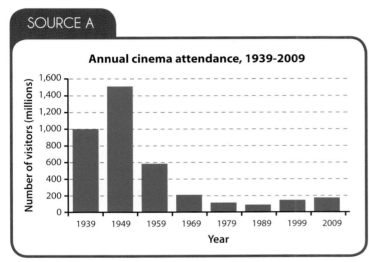

Annual cinema attendance, 1939-2009

Official figures from the Cinema Exhibitors' Association

SOURCE B

A range of films on offer at a multiplex cinema (2011)

Radio

The highly popular entertainment of the inter-war years continued to adapt to new audiences in the last decades of the twentieth century. Local commercial radio stations were allowed from 1973. In the next 20 years, many local stations were founded, providing competition for the radio channels of the BBC. The sheer versatility of radio means that, while it will never regain its influence of the early years of the twentieth century, it still remains an integral part of life for many people in Wales and England.

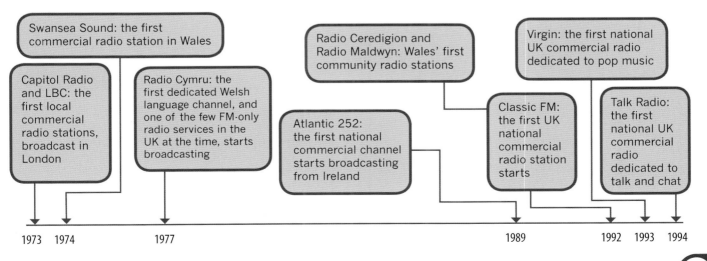

Swansea Sound: the first commercial radio station in Wales

Capitol Radio and LBC: the first local commercial radio stations, broadcast in London

Radio Cymru: the first dedicated Welsh language channel, and one of the few FM-only radio services in the UK at the time, starts broadcasting

Radio Ceredigion and Radio Maldwyn: Wales' first community radio stations

Atlantic 252: the first national commercial channel starts broadcasting from Ireland

Classic FM: the first UK national commercial radio station starts

Virgin: the first national UK commercial radio dedicated to pop music

Talk Radio: the first national UK commercial radio dedicated to talk and chat

1973   1974   1977   1989   1992   1993   1994

Radio landmarks during the late twentieth century

Almost 90% of the UK population are regularly tuning into the radio, according to the latest industry figures. They reveal that in the last quarter of 2009, 46 million adults listened to their favourite radio station each week. At the same time radio listening via mobile phone is continuing to grow steadily. The research shows that 6.7 million listeners tuned in this way during the last three months of 2009 – up by half a million from the same time last year

From a report by government regulator OFCOM (2010)

DEVELOPMENTS IN ENTERTAINMENT TECHNOLOGY

In the late 1970s, video games like *Pong* and *Space Invaders* became highly popular. These were the forerunners of modern video games and helped the new entertainment industry to expand hugely.

In the 1990s the range of entertainment offered by **home computers** began to challenge the dominance of television as the most popular modern form of entertainment. Sophisticated games, information, news, music and film were all available on CD-ROMs, DVDs or increasingly through the Internet. Towards the end of the first decade of the twenty-first century, home video consoles like *Play Station*, *Xbox* and *Wii* were increasingly entertaining new generations of people.

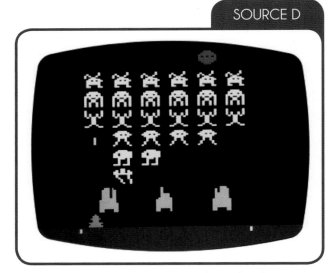

Screen of a Space Invaders *game, launched in the late 1970s*

More and more people accessed television through the Internet, and mobile phones with multiple applications were also becoming more common. Another growth area, particularly among young people, was the **social networking** sites, chat rooms and Internet gaming sites.

WOW! WE CAN GET MOVIES VIA COMPUTER! LET'S THROW OUT OUR T.V. !

WOW! WE CAN GET THE INTERNET ON T.V.! LET'S THROW OUT OUR COMPUTER!

SCHWADRn

Reproduced by permission of www.cartoonstock.com

A cartoon published in a magazine (2007)

Facebook is where I keep up with what my kids are doing. I am amazed at the number of times they get tagged in picture albums. Their whole adolescent history is being documented in photographs on the site. Not that they always want me to see!

Steve Rayson, an IT consultant, in an online vote for the Learning Tools Compendium (2008)

SOURCE G

The Internet has had some bad press in the past. In its earlier days the impression was given that Net surfers were sad, friendless nerds who would be better off turning their attention to getting a life. Nothing could be further from the truth. The Internet has something to offer everyone irrespective of their age, sex, education or interests. And the good news is that not only is it getting bigger and better all the time, but it's getting cheaper and easier to use. There has never been a better time to start taking part in the greatest communications revolution since the advent of television.

Terry Burrows, an author of self-help manuals, writing in The Internet Made Painless *(2001)*

TASKS

1. Explain why cinema attendances began to rise again by the 1990s.

2. Look at Source A. How useful is this source to an historian studying the history of the cinema?

3. What does Source B show you about cinemas in the twenty first century?

4. Describe the main developments in radio since the 1970s.

5. Would the author of Source F agree with the view of the Internet expressed in Source G?

6. Discuss the following view: 'The most important influence on entertainment since the 1970s has been the development of the Internet.'

Examination practice

This section provides guidance on how to answer questions 2(b) and 3(b) from Units 1 and 2. The question is worth 5 marks.

Questions 2(b) and 3(b) – the understanding of key features through the selection of appropriate knowledge

Describe how pop music has helped to raise money for charity. [5 marks]

Tips on how to answer

- Make sure you only include information that is **directly relevant**.
- Jot down your initial thoughts, making a list of the points you intend to mention.
- After you have finished your list try to put the points into **chronological order** by numbering them.
- It is a good idea to start your answer using the words from the question. E.g.: 'Pop music has helped to raise a lot of money for charity...'
- Try to include **specific factual details** such as dates, events, and the names of key people. The more informed your description the higher the mark you will receive.
- Aim to write at least **two full-length paragraphs**.

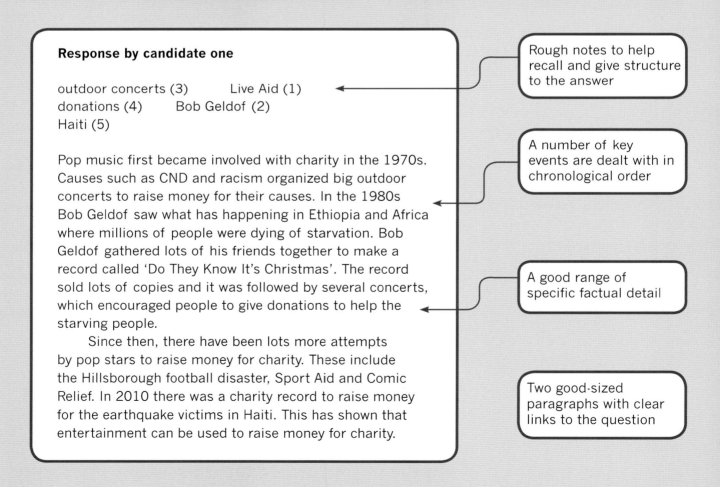

Response by candidate one

outdoor concerts (3)   Live Aid (1)
donations (4)   Bob Geldof (2)
Haiti (5)

Pop music first became involved with charity in the 1970s. Causes such as CND and racism organized big outdoor concerts to raise money for their causes. In the 1980s Bob Geldof saw what has happening in Ethiopia and Africa where millions of people were dying of starvation. Bob Geldof gathered lots of his friends together to make a record called 'Do They Know It's Christmas'. The record sold lots of copies and it was followed by several concerts, which encouraged people to give donations to help the starving people.

Since then, there have been lots more attempts by pop stars to raise money for charity. These include the Hillsborough football disaster, Sport Aid and Comic Relief. In 2010 there was a charity record to raise money for the earthquake victims in Haiti. This has shown that entertainment can be used to raise money for charity.

Rough notes to help recall and give structure to the answer

A number of key events are dealt with in chronological order

A good range of specific factual detail

Two good-sized paragraphs with clear links to the question

This is a very useful answer. It contains relevant information, which is focused on answering the question set. There are specific factual details including dates, events and the names of specific charity campaigns connected with pop music.

The answer reaches the highest level and gains maximum marks (5).

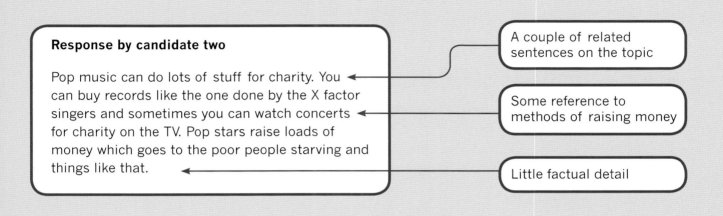

Response by candidate two

Pop music can do lots of stuff for charity. You can buy records like the one done by the X factor singers and sometimes you can watch concerts for charity on the TV. Pop stars raise loads of money which goes to the poor people starving and things like that.

A couple of related sentences on the topic

Some reference to methods of raising money

Little factual detail

Examiner's comment

This answer demonstrates some knowledge of how pop music can raise money for charity. It does try to answer the question and deserves credit for this. However, it is quite brief and lacks specific knowledge about the topic such as key figures, events, charitable causes and amount of money raised.

There are only a few related facts and the answer is placed in the lowest level gaining 2 marks.

Now you have a go

Describe the development of S4C in Wales.   [5 marks]

CHAPTER 7

WHAT OPPORTUNITIES FOR PEOPLE TO HAVE HOLIDAYS WERE THERE IN THE FIRST HALF OF THE TWENTIETH CENTURY?

TRADITIONAL HOLIDAY RESORTS

Around 1900 the idea of a 'holiday' as we see it was still beginning to grow. The growth of the railway network in the later nineteenth century had linked up the coast to the major urban centres, and seaside resorts had begun to develop to meet the needs of a new group – the **tourist**.

Traditional seaside resorts

By 1900 that great British institution, the family holiday, was developing. The **Bank Holiday Act** of 1871 had given all workers an extra six days off a year and these were often spent on visits to the seaside. Annual paid holidays were still at the discretion of employers, but were becoming more common by

the turn of the century. For example, in 1897 the Amalgamated Society of Railway Servants persuaded the railway companies to give their workers a week's paid holiday after five year's service.

Seaside resorts had grown in the nineteenth century to cater for the needs of tourists. These were all within a day's easy travel from the big industrial towns and cities. Some, like Margate, Southport or Llandudno, set out to attract the richer clients from the professional classes, while those like Southend or Blackpool were aimed at the less well off. Richer families stayed in large hotels with names like the Grand, the Imperial or the Regent. Other holidaymakers stayed in **boarding houses** that offered 'rooms and attendance': they brought their own food, which the landlady cooked for them.

The Strand Hotel in Brighton, around 1900

Holiday life in these resorts was centred on the beach. Popular activities included:
- Bathing and paddling;
- Donkey rides;
- Punch and Judy shows;
- Walking on the pier;
- Strolling on the promenade.

Spas and inland resorts

In Wales many well-off people visited the **spa towns** of mid-Wales: Llandrindod Wells, Builth Wells, Llanwrtyd Wells and Llangammarch Wells. They also visited the mountains of north Wales, where the Snowdon Mountain Railway had opened in 1896.

Tourists enjoying a Punch and Judy show on the promenade at Rhyl in 1910

After 1880, hotels, apartments, new spa treatment centres, two pavilions, a golf course, bowling and putting greens and a 14 acre boating lake were all built to cater for as many as 80,000 visitors a year. These mainly wealthy visitors arrived from all over the land, bringing with them their own entourage of servants who further swelled the numbers in the town. Local papers listed week by week the names of visitors to Llandrindod Wells, reflecting the importance not only of being there, but of being seen to be there. The growth of the town continued unabated into the early years of the 20th Century, with the railway at one stage running through trains to destinations as far apart as London, Birmingham, Manchester and Liverpool.

From a tourist information guide to Llandrindod Wells in Powys (2008)

Day excursions

Poorer people didn't have the time or money for long holidays, but chapels or clubs would organize day trips by **charabanc** (motor coach) or train. For workers in south Wales, trips to Barry Island, Porthcawl or across to Somerset by steamboat were popular. In North Wales, Rhyl and Prestatyn served the same purpose. If trips to the seaside proved too expensive or difficult, a visit to a local beauty spot or whinberry picking on the mountains was still a welcome break from the toil of working life.

As children we were lucky that our father worked for the Great Western Railway so we had privilege tickets to travel. We could not have afforded to go otherwise. So we went on holidays to Burnham on Sea, Porthcawl, Ilfracombe, Penzance, Weston super Mare and Barry. We played on the beach, bathed and watched the Punch and Judy shows. And there were **Pierrots** too, playing on the sand.

Florence Amor, who was born in 1897, remembering her family holidays in the years before the First World War

Holidays abroad for the well-to-do

One class of people had long enjoyed the experience of a holiday. The rich were great travellers, visiting resorts such as Hove and Torquay on the south coast of England where it cost about £25 a week to rent a house.

SOURCE E

The railway now runs all the way from Geneva to the foot of the Simplon Mountain, an easy journey of less than eight hours. Then there is really almost a continuous terrace all along the shore of the lake from Lausanne to Villeneuve of hotels like palaces, one more magnificent than another, with terraces and gardens, and fountains and bands of music, and such luxurious public apartments, and sumptuous banquets. For the last few years there has been a perfect insane rush of the whole tourist world to these parts of Switzerland.

Fanny Kemble, a British actress and author, writing in a letter to a family member in 1889

SOURCE F

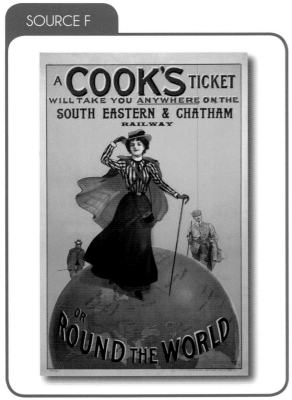

An advertisement aimed at attracting tourists (1910)

There was an excellent train service throughout Europe and continental spots such as Monte Carlo, Venice and Switzerland were popular destinations for the better off. A **'European tour'** was considered an essential experience for rich young people who had just finished schooling.

TASKS

1. Explain why seaside resorts were popular places to visit in the early twentieth century.
2. How useful is Source B to an historian studying holidays in the early twentieth century?
3. Use Source C and your own knowledge to explain the growth of the spa towns of Mid Wales.
4. How far does Source E support the view that only richer people enjoyed foreign travel

NEW DEVELOPMENTS IN HOLIDAY PATTERNS IN THE 1920s AND 1930s

The period after the First World War saw many changes in holiday patterns in England and Wales. As the economy of the UK suffered in the 1920s and early 1930s, people increasingly saw breaks and holidays as a vital part of their lifestyle, important for their health and happiness. In Germany, the Nazi government encouraged the 'Strength through Joy' movement, which urged Germans to make better use of their leisure time. The same attitude to leisure filtered down into the UK where the seaside continued to be the main draw. On August Bank Holiday Monday in 1937 over 500,000 people visited Blackpool in trains, coaches and cars.

Time off and holiday pay

Despite the impact of the Depression years, more and more people found that they could afford a break. Holidays with pay had been introduced for many workers in the years between 1919 and 1922. By 1929 three million workers were receiving at least one week's holiday with pay. In 1938 the government passed an act that gave all workers a holiday with pay for the first time. Figures suggest that over 5 million people enjoyed a week's holiday in 1939. In South Wales, **'miners' week'** saw many workers and their families visiting the resorts of Barry and Porthcawl. In the north of England, **'wakes week'** saw similar moves to the coast by workers from the mill towns.

Charabancs and private cars

In the period between the wars, a great boost to holidays came with advances in road transport. This opened new destinations and new kinds of holidays to tourists. Trains still remained the most common form of travel, but more people preferred coaches and even motor cars. Charabanc excursions allowed trippers to visit more remote regions such as the Llŷn Peninsula and Pembrokeshire, areas that were not served well by rail. More families were able to save for a car in the 1930s and these were commonly used for outings and holidays. Even though there were around 2 millions cars on the road in 1939, it should be remembered that seven out of eight families still didn't own a car. There were also around half a million motorcycles around, many with sidecars that could take a partner or a small family.

Tourists arriving at Blackpool station on August Bank Holiday Monday in 1937

The Holidays With Pay Act (1938) marked the end of a twenty-year campaign for paid leisure time. The Act allowed one week's annual paid vacation to all full-time workers. The Act marked an important moment in British history. The campaign for paid holidays helped to create a market for mass leisure and tourism.

Sandra Dawson, a university professor, writing in an on-line article, The Campaign for Holidays with pay *(2007)*

There were day trips organized by the local club down to Penarth or Porthcawl by charabanc. I was so young at the time, I didn't realise why the bus stopped so many times and all the men got out.

John Prior, of Porth in south Wales, remembering going on day trips in the 1930s

Changes at the seaside

The seaside attractions of the earlier part of the century remained big draws, but there were some developments that added to the appeal of the family holiday. Most holidaymakers still stayed in small guesthouses or boarding houses. These now began to offer 'full board' (all meals included) or even the new **'bed and breakfast'**. Guesthouses were often strictly run and their landladies became the butt of comedians' jokes in shows at the end of the piers.

Popular 1930s end-of-pier jokes poking fun at landladies

Ron Saunders describing a family holiday in 1936, in the BBC television series The Tourist *(1984)*

Traditional seaside entertainment – the pier, paddling, Punch and Judy, promenading – remained popular. Some resorts tried to tempt tourists with new attractions like ice-rinks or open air swimming pools, often called lidos. The first big open air pool was opened in Blackpool in 1923 at a cost of £100,000. Soon every resort had to have one. Health and fitness classes, beauty contests and water carnivals were among the activities that took place at the pool. The Cold Knap complex was laid out in Barry and the resorts of Porthcawl, Rhyl and Llandudno were all upgraded. The 'tourist industry' was growing with its fish and chip shops, fairgrounds, dancehalls and souvenir shops.

SOURCE F

The lido complex in Ebbw Vale, 1930s

Contrary to the advice we get today, sunbathing and getting a suntan was encouraged. Chemists began to sell suntan cream and lotions. It also became fashionable to wear rubber bathing caps. Bathing costumes were still all in one but now began to show off arms and legs!

SOURCE G

An advertisement for a trip to the seaside by train in the 1930s

Hiking, cycling and camping

The 1930s saw people starting to take hiking and cycling breaks in the countryside across the UK. Walking and cycling clubs were formed all over the country. **The Youth Hostel Association** was established in 1930 to cater for the needs of these tourists. It built hostels to provide cheap, clean accommodation for hikers, cyclists and other visitors to the countryside. By 1939 there were over 300 hostels each charging around 1 shilling (5p) a night.

Camping also grew in popularity. Many youngsters made their own tents out of sacks and camped on nearby mountains or by streams. Old railway carriages were another new holiday development. They were kitted out as camping coaches and situated at country railway stations or by the sea. They cost about £4 a week to hire.

Holiday camps

The large profits to be made out of tourism led to the growth of specialised holiday companies that catered for a mass market. In the late 1930s this saw the emergence of the **holiday camp**. Holiday camps were not a new idea, but a businessman called Billy Butlin took them to a new level. Inspired by his experience of a wet weekend in Barry, when he saw families kept out of their boarding houses during the day, Butlin opened his first holiday camp at Skegness on the Lincolnshire coast in 1936. It cost as little as £2 10d (£2.50) per person per week including all meals, activities and entertainment. Butlins' slogan was *'A week's holiday for a week's pay'*. The camps were very popular with families, because they were much more relaxed than many hotels and guesthouses. Butlins' Redcoats organized games and competitions such as knobbly knees, glamorous grannies and talent shows. By 1939, there were nearly 200 holiday camps in Wales and England, and over 500,000 people had enjoyed a holiday at a camp. However, the peak times for holiday camps were to come after the Second World War.

It is important to remember that while holidays and breaks were becoming more common, there were still a great many people who had to make do with a day-trip or nothing at all. But increasingly people were beginning to realise the value of a break from their daily routine.

We never had enough money for a proper holiday. But Mam and Dad would take us up the mountain to search for whinberries. Up we would go with our jam jars. We would make a day of it and take some sandwiches and a bottle of lemonade. Mam would then make a tart for Sunday.

Mostyn Davies from Llanybydder in West Wales, remembering how his family spent their holiday time in the 1930s

TASKS

1. What does Source A tell you about seaside resorts in the 1930s?

2. How useful is Source G to an historian studying holidays in the 1930s?

3. How far does Source K support the view that many people were unable to go on holiday at this time?

4. Describe the setting up of the first holiday camps.

Examination practice

This section provides guidance on how to answer questions 2(c) and 3(c) from Units 1 and 2. The question carries 8 marks in total but is sub-divided in 2 × 4-mark questions.

Questions 2(c) and 3(c) – the selection of knowledge and the explanation of key features

Explain why holiday camps were popular with many holidaymakers. [4 marks]

Tips on how to answer

- Aim to give a variety of reasons that are **well supported** and **developed**.
- The **more reasons** you can mention the better your chances of scoring the higher marks.
- Most importantly, these reasons need to be supported with **relevant factual detail**.
- Avoid generalised comments, as these will gain you low marks.
- Always support your statements with **examples**.
- Make sure the information you include is **directly relevant**.
  E.g. Does it answer the question?

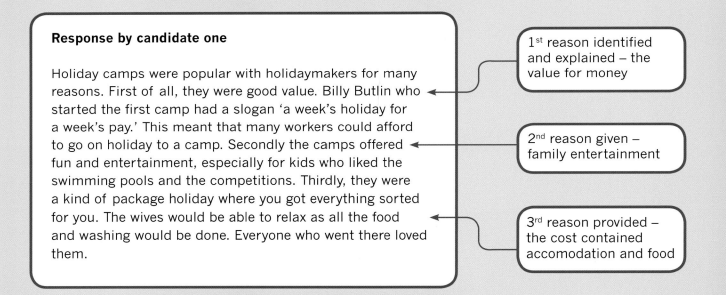

Response by candidate one

Holiday camps were popular with holidaymakers for many reasons. First of all, they were good value. Billy Butlin who started the first camp had a slogan 'a week's holiday for a week's pay.' This meant that many workers could afford to go on holiday to a camp. Secondly the camps offered fun and entertainment, especially for kids who liked the swimming pools and the competitions. Thirdly, they were a kind of package holiday where you got everything sorted for you. The wives would be able to relax as all the food and washing would be done. Everyone who went there loved them.

1st reason identified and explained – the value for money

2nd reason given – family entertainment

3rd reason provided – the cost contained accomodation and food

Examiner's comment

The answer identifies a number of specific reasons and these are supported with good knowledge. There is a clear focus on the question set. The last sentence is a generalisation but the answer reaches Level 2 and is worthy of maximum [4] marks.

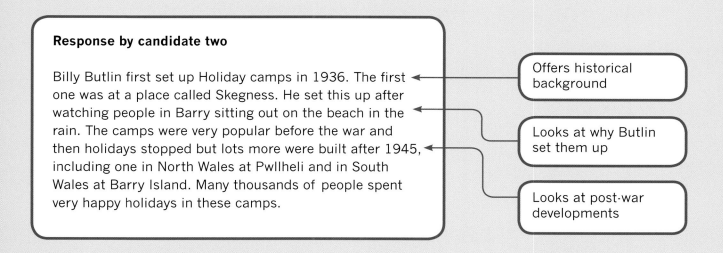

Response by candidate two

Billy Butlin first set up Holiday camps in 1936. The first one was at a place called Skegness. He set this up after watching people in Barry sitting out on the beach in the rain. The camps were very popular before the war and then holidays stopped but lots more were built after 1945, including one in North Wales at Pwllheli and in South Wales at Barry Island. Many thousands of people spent very happy holidays in these camps.

Offers historical background

Looks at why Butlin set them up

Looks at post-war developments

Examiner's comment

The candidate has lots of knowledge about holiday camps but does not use this to answer the question set. It is a descriptive type of response and does not address the issue of why the camps were popular. This has to be placed in Level 1, getting 2 marks due to the useful knowledge of the subject deployed.

Now you have a go

Explain why families were attracted to seaside resorts in the eary twentieth century. [4 marks]

CHAPTER 8

HOW MUCH DID TOURISM AND HOLIDAY PATTERNS IN WALES AND ENGLAND CHANGE IN THE 1950s AND 1960s?

SNOWDON
from Llyn Llydaw
NORTH WALES

Lake District

owdonia

Brecon Beacons

shire

THE HIGH POINT OF BRITISH HOLIDAYS, 1945-1965

During the Second World War landmines had been buried on many of Britain's beaches and they were therfore closed to the public. After the war, the mines were cleared and the crowds returned. Most of the resorts and the types of holiday that had been popular in the 1930s continued to attract tourists after the war. However, it is important to remember that by 1950 holidays were not yet a regular part of family life.

SOURCE A

British families that spent holidays away from home	50%
British families that had occasional day trips	9%
British families that never went away from home	41%

A survey conducted by the British Tourist Board in 1948

SOURCE B

I don't remember holidays being that important. No one asked you where you'd been when you went back to school in September. Sometimes we went to stay with relatives. My uncle lived in Brighton and when we visited him that was the first time that I'd seen the sea. Other times we went on day trips on the bus. Because we lived in the Midlands we could go anywhere really. I remember going to Cheltenham, Weston-super-Mare and Wicksteed Park in Kettering where they had a park with swings and big slides. We never went to a hotel or anything because we couldn't afford it.

A woman born during the war, remembering her holidays as a young girl in the early 1950s

However, the situation was changing and there were new developments that would have an impact on the typical British family holiday in the next 20 years. In many ways the decades after 1950 became the high point of the 'great British family holiday'.

Reasons for the growth in holidays after 1945

- Relief at the end of the war;
- Better wages after the war;
- More people entitled to holidays with pay;
- Better road transport;
- Growth of holiday camps;
- Popularity of caravan holidays;
- Better advertising and selling of holidays.

Holiday opportunities

During the 1950s and 1960s, living standards in Wales and England rose steadily. In 1959 the Prime Minister, Harold Macmillan said that people in the UK had 'never had it so good'. One area where people chose to spend their money was in going on holiday.

Caravans

Holidays in caravans really took off after the war. Caravans had once been the plaything of a privileged minority but after the Second World War they went on to become a firm favourite with over a quarter of British holidaymakers.

Caravans gradually became a source of cheap holidays especially on the growing number of **caravan sites** dotted around the country.

Caravan parks mushroomed along large stretches of the coastline such as Towyn in north Wales and Porthcawl in south Wales. Trecco Bay became one of Europe's largest caravan parks.

These caravan parks often became more like holiday camps. However, unlike a holiday camp the facilities were not always 'all in'. You could pay per week for membership of a social club including use of the swimming pool, licensed club bar, games room and entertainment. Touring caravanning also grew far beyond the level experienced in the pre-war years.

Trecco Bay caravan park in the 1950s

Changes in caravanning reflected wider changes in British society, in particular the increased availability of cars, but also the improved road network and changing attitudes towards holidaymaking and leisure time. Caravans provided independence and the freedom of the open road – the chance to explore hidden corners of Britain and abroad while keeping their home comforts in tow. For many women in particular, the caravan holiday had social benefits providing escape from home life and even emancipation.

TASKS

1. How far does Source A support the view that holidays were an important part of people's lives after the Second World War?

2. Explain why there was a growth in the number of people going on holidays after 1945.

3. Describe the growth in caravan holidays in the 1950s and 1960s.

4. How useful is Source G to an historian studying holidays in the 1950s and 1960s?

Holiday camps

Holiday camps remained particularly popular as a holiday choice. The golden age of the holiday camp was in the 1950s and 1960s. Many army camps left over after the war quickly became holiday camps. Other camps had been taken over by the military during the war and once again opened their doors to holidaymakers. In some cases, the campers moved in almost as soon as the soldiers moved out.

The holiday camp continued to provide what many holidaymakers were looking for. Prices were reasonable, food was plentiful for the time and there was plenty to do, even when it was raining.

A notable newcomer to the holiday camp scene in the late 1940s was Fred Pontin. His first holiday camp was at Brean Sands near Burnham-on-Sea in Somerset, which opened in 1946. By 1949 he had six camps in England. Pontin's camps were quite small by holiday camp standards, taking no more than 250 campers. This made Pontin's camps significantly different from Butlin's. Butlin's also continued to grow and further camps were added at Minehead (1962) and Barry Island (1966). An exciting modern feature of the camp at Minehead was a monorail. The monorail was considered a very modern form of transport in the 1960s.

The monorail at Butlin's in Minehead in 1969

By the late 1950s, there were hundreds of camps throughout the whole country. An annual publication *Holiday Camps – Directory and Magazine* listed many of them and described the facilities. In 1955, this form of holiday was so popular that the magazine encouraged people to book early and to avoid the popular months of July and August. It was felt that if people were to spread their holidays over the period from June to September, there would be less stress on the holiday industry and it might be better able to cope with the increasing numbers. Needless to say, the campaign failed and most people still took holidays in July and August.

A brochure for a holiday camp in the mid 1950s

What great times we had there. I remember the little chalets we had, with the loos and baths in a separate block! Radio Butlin's would wake you up in the morning ready to go to the dining hall. We were in Gloucester House and my Dad was on the house committee. I remember the monorail, which would stop over the swimming pool and the chair lifts that were really high. [I was a member of] The Butlin's Beaver Club... with all your Redcoat aunties and uncles who would take you off to be pirates for the day, or whatever activity was going on. At the end of the week there would be a sports day, with all the dads taking part. Our parents would only see us at mealtimes, as it was perfectly safe then to go off and do your own thing with your brothers and sisters. And yes, there were knobbly knees and glamorous granny competitions. Happy days!

A woman remembers visits to a holiday camp in the 1960s on an Internet message board. (2010)

Holiday camps inspired very different reactions amongst people. For some, a stay in one was almost unthinkable, for others they were the ideal holiday. Many thousands of people returned year after year to the big camps at Bognor, Barry Island and Skegness.

SOURCE E

The main complaint that was levelled against Butlin's by commentators at the time was that of "regimentation". The campers were essentially told how to have a good time and the Redcoats made sure they did. Regimentation or not, Butlin's was never quiet. Those who longed for remote, unspoilt Cornish villages would not have enjoyed Butlin's.

From the Internet site on Seaside holidays.co.uk (2007)

SOURCE F

Hello campers! We've got a fun packed programme for you today.
Holiday Princess competition
Knobbly Knees contest
Kiddies fancy dress
Bingo in the Hawaiian ballroom
Ugly Face competition in the Swiss bar

Gladys Pugh, a character in the popular 1980s television comedy, Hi De Hi, *which was based on life in a 1950s holiday camp*

TASKS

1. What does Source C tell you about holiday camps in the 1950s?

2. Why do Sources D and E have different views about the experience of holiday camps?

3. Describe the growth of Pontins holiday camps.

4. Why do you think the comedy series *Hi De Hi* was so popular in the 1980s?

THE IMPACT OF THE MOTOR CAR

One factor that had a huge influence on holiday patterns in the 1950s and 1960s was the growth of the motor car. Car ownership grew quickly after the war, as increased wages meant that more people could afford their own car. In 1939 there were 2.5 million cars registered in the UK: by 1963 this figure had trebled to 7.5 million. One in four families now owned a car and more women were passing the driving test. Even more people were now able to reach the holiday regions, taking trips to the country and to the coast. In the early 1960s, a wave of railway closures called the **Beeching Axe**, hit the country as the government decided that car and road transport was the future. Going on holiday was to change forever.

SOURCE A

In 1951, 47% of holidaymakers went by train to their destination, 27% went by bus or coach and 27% by private car. By 1959, nearly half of the total number of holidaymakers went by car and by 1969 nearly 70%.

Figures from the English Tourist Board

Seaside resorts began to adapt to cater for people in cars. New car parks were built, roadside cafes sprang up, and scenic drives around headlands were signposted. New attractions were thought of to entice motorists into the resorts. Hotels and guesthouses without car parks began to lose business. New accommodation catering for the motorist was built, often called **motels**.

A vast £1 million development scheme is behind the remarkable transformation of Aberavon Beach – a scheme to turn a barren beach into the best seaside resort in Wales. The question is, will people come to a steel-making town for their holidays?

We think the mounting number of visitors in their motor cars and the growing popularity of the beach gives a clear answer. Things look good for Port Talbot as a holiday destination.

Part of an advertising feature in the Western Mail *newspaper (1960)*

SOURCE C

The West Shore beach, Walney Island, Barrow in Furness, in the 1950s

SOURCE D

Caravan manufacturer Sam Alper opened the first Little Chef in Reading in 1958 after seeing roadside diners on a trip to the United States. With only 11 seats it was a tiny start for the chain. But the formula of good food in bright clean surroundings was an instant success and Alper opened more branches. At its peak there were more than 400 Little Chefs around the country.

From an article on the 50th anniversary of the Little Chef diners in the Daily Mirror *newspaper (2008)*

SOURCE E

In 1967 we had a family holiday to Swanage in Dorset. We left home after breakfast and soon made it over the Severn Bridge. After that things slowed down. I'll always remember those traffic jams – Warminster, Shaftesbury, Blandford Forum – hours spent going nowhere. We got out and walked faster than my father drove the car. The next year we went to Cornwall, but we drove through the night this time.

A woman from South Wales, remembering traffic jams in the west of England in the 1960s (2010)

Of course, the growth in use of the motor car meant problems. Negative issues included noise and overcrowded roads especially in the towns and resorts, which had never been constructed to cope with motor cars. Some of the routes to the coast became notorious for bottlenecks and town planners began to dream up bypasses and ring roads.

TASKS

1. Explain why the growth of the motor car changed holiday patterns in the 1950s.

2. How useful is Source A to an historian studying holidays in the 1950s?

3. Use Source D and your own knowledge to explain how businesses adapted for holidaymakers in cars.

4. Describe the problems caused by increased car use.

5. 'The biggest influence on holidays in the 1950s and 1960s was the growth of car ownership.' Do you agree with this view?

THE NEED FOR NATIONAL PARKS

People were also encouraged to look away from the coast for holidays and breaks. In 1947, a Government committee proposed **national parks** to conserve areas of fine scenery. 1949 was a landmark year as the government passed an Act of Parliament to establish National Parks to preserve and enhance their natural beauty and provide recreational opportunities for the public. Lewis Silkin, Minister for Town and Country Planning, described it as "the most exciting Act of the post-war Parliament".

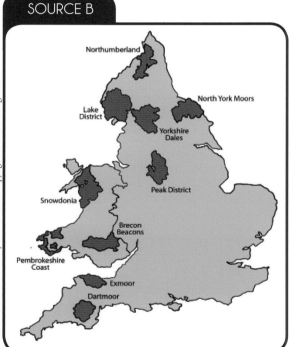

The location of the National Parks created in the 1950s

Ramblers on a hike in the countryside in the 1950s

SOURCE A

The essential requirements of a National Park are that it should have great natural beauty and a high value for open-air recreation. Selected areas should be quickly accessible from each of the main centres of population in England and Wales. There is merit in variety and it would be wrong to confine the selection of National Parks to the more rugged areas of mountain and moorland, and to exclude other districts which, though of less outstanding grandeur and wildness, have their own distinctive beauty and a high recreational value.

Sir Arthur Hobhouse, chairman of the government committee on establishing national parks, explaining the criteria for selection (1947)

SOURCE C

A footpath and signpost in a National Park

The National Parks began with the Peak District in 1951. By the end of the decade the Lake District, Snowdonia, Dartmoor, Pembrokeshire Coast, North York Moors, Yorkshire Dales, Exmoor, Northumberland and Brecon Beacons National Parks had also been established. These areas promoted rural tourism through activities such as pony-trekking, canoeing and outdoor pursuits.

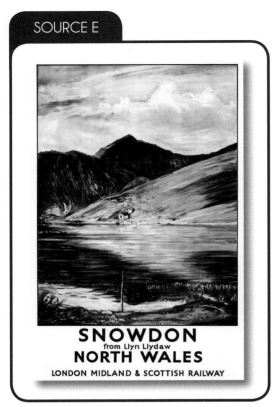

SNOWDON
from Llyn Llydaw
NORTH WALES
LONDON MIDLAND & SCOTTISH RAILWAY

A railway company advertisement for holidays in one of the newly created national parks

National parks were a big success in attracting visitors and holidaymakers in the 1950s and 1960s. Even though not many of the areas were well served by railways, especially after the Beeching axe of 1963, the growth of car ownership brought them within easy reach of holidaymakers and day-trippers. Later problems such as congestion and erosion were not yet apparent.

I think of the Peak District in connection to the happy hiking days of my youth. A gang of us would board the train at the station in Sheffield and head off to Castleton. How I loved to go up to Winnets Pass and sit and have fun flirting with the lads – it made our trip all the more exciting. Castleton for me is a lovely memory of a carefree youth, fresh air and roaming those lush green hills in the 1950s. It is years since I was there but the memory is still as fresh now as if it was only yesterday – great times!

A woman posting a message on the Friends Reunited message board (2008)

TASKS

1. What does Source E tell you about holidays in National Parks in the 1950s?
2. Explain why National Parks were popular places to visit.
3. Use Source A and your own knowledge to explain why National Parks were set up.
4. How useful is Source F to an historian studying the setting up of National Parks?
5. Why was the car important in creating tourism in National Parks?

Examination practice

This section provides guidance on how to answer questions 2(d) and 3(d)) from Units 1 and 2. This is an extended answer question that provides a scaffold to help you structure your answer. The question carries 10 marks.

Questions 2(d) and 3(d) – using own knowledge to construct a two-sided essay

Was the growth of caravan parks the most important development in tourism in the UK during the 1950s and 1960s? Explain your answer fully. [10 marks]

You should give a two-sided answer to this question:
 - *discuss the growth of caravan parks in the 1950s and 1960s;*
 - *discuss other factors that caused tourism to grow;*
 - *give a judgement.*

Tips on how to answer

● You need to develop a **two-sided** answer that is balanced and well supported.

● You should start by discussing the **factor mentioned in the question**, using your factual knowledge to explain why this factor is important.

● You then need to consider the **counter-argument** by using your knowledge to examine other relevant factors.

● These points need to be discussed in some detail, starting a new paragraph for each point.

● Aim to link the paragraphs by using words such as 'other factors include', 'also important', 'in addition to', 'however'.

● **Avoid generalised comments** – the more specific your observations the higher the mark you will get, providing the factual information is relevant to the question.

● **Conclude** your answer with a **link back** to the question, making a judgement about the importance of the factor listed in the question when ranked against the other factors you have discussed.

● You should aim to write between one and two sides of a page.

Candidate response

Caravan parks were a very important development in UK tourism during the 1950s and 1960s. Holidays in caravans really took off after the war. They were cheap holidays and were popular because people didn't have much money. A family could hire a caravan on a caravan site by the seaside. There were big caravan parks in north Wales and in south Wales. Trecco Bay became one of Europe's largest caravan parks. These caravan parks were like holiday camps with swimming pools, bars, games and entertainment.

Introduction that links to the question

Deals with the key factor mentioned in the question

Provides some detail to support the argument

However, caravan parks were not the most important development to affect tourism during the 1950s and 1960s. The most important development has to be the growth of the motor car. Without this people wouldn't have been able to get to their caravans. The car was much more affordable in the 1950s and with it tourists could go to more places, at the seaside and in the new national Parks. Lots of places now began to cater for tourists in cars. Hotels built car parks and cafes were opened on the main roads. The car did cause problems though as there were huge traffic jams and bottlenecks created on the way to the seaside.

Another really important development was the holiday camp. These had been given to the army during the war but after the war the army moved out and the tourists moved in. Butlins and Pontins opened holiday camps all over the country and millions of people went on holiday there. These camps were 'all-in'. Some people didn't like the camps but they didn't have to go there. Those that went loved them.

So, the biggest development in the 1950s and 1960s had to be the growth of the motor car. Without this the holidaymakers would not have been able to go to new places, especially after lots of railways closed in the 1960s. Caravan parks were popular and so were holiday camps but the car was the biggest change.

> Begins the counter-argument. Using the term 'however' makes it clear you are now looking at other factors

> Other factors are discussed such as the motor car and the holiday camps

> A new paragraph is started for each new factor

> A good reasoned conclusion that provides a clear judgement linked back to the question

Examiner's comment

This is an impressive answer. It is a reasoned and supported two-sided account with a good balance. It displays accurate and relevant historical detail and the quality of written communication is very good. It clearly evaluates the issue in the question and reaches a clear judgement. Under examination conditions this would reach Level 4, and gain the maximum 10 marks.

Now you have a go

Was the opening of national parks the most important development in tourism in the UK during the 1950s and 1960s? Explain your answer fully. [10 marks]

You should give a two-sided answer to this question:
- *discuss the opening of national parks in the 1950s and 1960s;*
- *discuss other factors that caused tourism to grow;*
- *give a judgement.*

CHAPTER 9

HOW FAR HAVE TOURISM AND HOLIDAY PATTERNS IN WALES AND ENGLAND CHANGED SINCE THE 1960s?

THE INCREASING USE OF AIR TRAVEL

By the late 1960s, competition from new kinds of holiday destinations abroad, together with changing tastes and expectations, began to affect the traditional family holiday destinations in the UK. Even then recent research has suggested that the impact on British resorts was perhaps not as great as was feared or predicted at the time.

Year	1971	1976	1981	1986	1991	1996
In the UK	34	38	37	31	33	35
Abroad	8	9	13	18	21	24
Total	42	47	50	49	54	59

Official tourist board figures showing holidays taken by UK tourists (figures in millions)

Package holidays to foreign destinations

The biggest change to British holiday patterns in this period was caused by the growth of cheaper **air travel**. From the late 1960s, holidays to the Mediterranean in particular became increasingly available and grew in popularity. The Mediterranean could offer the guaranteed sun that British resorts could not. Trips to Europe had always been popular with better-off tourists and independent travellers often seeking peace and quiet and isolation, but by the 1970s whole stretches of the coast of southern Europe had become geared to **mass tourism**.

SOURCE C

The former fishing village of Benidorm photographed in the 1930s and 1980s

Prices to the Mediterranean were extremely competitive and travel agents began to offer **package holidays** where the holiday price included both the airfare and accommodation. Ironically, holiday camp bosses like Fred Pontin were also responsible for helping to start the foreign package holiday craze in the 1960s when his company funded the construction of a new hotel in Sardinia. Pontins offered a two week holiday with flights, accommodation, food, drink, entertainment and guaranteed sun for less than £50 a head. The venture was successful and Pontinental Holidays was formed to build additional hotels in Majorca, Spain and Ibiza. The attraction of the foreign holiday became irresistible to many families.

Many early package holidaymakers travelled by coach or train, but during the 1970s the jet aircraft became the standard form of transport to the sun. Most people travelling from Wales by air flew from airports in England, but Cardiff International Airport, based at Rhoose, developed rapidly, handling international flights to more destinations. In the late 1970s, the businessman Sir Freddie Laker drove down flight prices with his 'no-frills' *Skytrain*, which offered cheap flights to America. Unfortunately Laker Airways went bust in 1982 but Laker had pioneered the way for modern low budget airlines such as Easyjet and Ryanair. As the twentieth century neared its close, holiday destinations had spread well beyond Europe.

Sir Freddie Laker launching his Skytrain service
from London Gatwick to New York in 1979

Around 10 million British people took a holiday abroad in 1979. Of these about 50% took a package tour. Spain is still most popular but catching up is the USA, attracting a million British tourists for the first time. Three things have brought this about – cheap airfares, the fall in value of the dollar and skilled marketing.

From a holiday survey carried out by the
Daily Mirror *newspaper (1980)*

TASKS

1. How useful is Source A to an historian studying changing holiday patterns from 1971-1996?

2. Explain why package holidays to the Mediterranean became popular in the 1970s.

3. How far does Source D back up the view that many people went on holiday to Spain because it had better weather?

4. Use Sources B and C to explain what had happened to many Spanish resorts by the 1970s.

5. Use Sources E and F to explain why Freddie Laker was important to the tourism industry.

The impact of the package holiday

The tourists who went to continental Europe were part of a great social change that still carries on today. Foreign travel had a great cultural impact. Experiences abroad have led to lifestyle changes in the UK. People began to experiment with foreign cooking at home and continental restaurants become popular as people try to relive their holiday diet in the UK. Clothing began to alter as people wore sunhats and shorts more regularly. Tourists brought home souvenirs to remind them of their experiences. Planes landed at Cardiff with tourists clutching sombreros and toy donkeys. There was a big impact on the British tourist industry, which had to adapt quickly and also a dramatic change in the small coastal villages of the Mediterranean and beyond that had to cater for the influx of holidaymakers from abroad.

Spain was very different back in 1970; it really was a foreign country, not an extension of Britain in the sun as it is in some places today. There were no 'English' pubs, no fish and chip shops, not even sausage, egg and bacon for breakfast and if you wanted English beer you were out of luck because you couldn't even get Watney's Red Barrel until about 1971. But it was a completely new experience for us all. I vividly remember a Cockney girl running into the sea in Majorca on her first day on holiday shouting to her friend. "Here 'Chelle, is this the life or wot?" And you know something? She was right, because holidays were never the same again once you got a taste of Spain. And Spanish resorts were about to change too.

*Paul Delplanque, a journalist writing about holidays in Spain
around 1970, in the* Teeside Evening Gazette *(September 2009)*

Oh this year I'm off to Sunny Spain,
Y Viva España.
I'm taking the Costa Brava 'plane,
Y Viva España.
If you'd like to chat a matador, in some cool cabana
And meet senoritas by the score,
España por favor.

Chorus of a UK hit song by Sylvia, Y Viva España (August 1974)

Yes I quite agree. I mean what's the point of being treated like sheep. What's the point of going abroad if you're just another tourist carted around in buses surrounded by sweaty mindless oafs from Kettering and Coventry in their cloth caps and their cardigans and their transistor radios and their Sunday Mirrors, complaining about the tea – "Oh they don't make it properly here, do they, not like at home" – and stopping at Majorcan bodegas selling fish and chips and Watney's Red Barrel and calamares and two veg and sitting in their cotton frocks squirting Timothy White's suncream all over their puffy raw swollen flesh 'cos they "overdid it on the first day."

A tourist speaking in a Monty Python television comedy sketch poking fun at package holidays (1971)

A cartoon of a Spanish resort in the 1990s

Reproduced by permission of www.cartoonstock.com

TASKS

1. Describe the impact that foreign package holidays had on the lifestyle of many British people in the 1970s.

2. Look at Source B. Can lyrics from popular songs ever be useful to historians?

3. Look at Sources A and C. Why do these sources say different things about package holidays?

4. What point is the cartoonist trying to make in Source D?

5. 'Package holidays had a bad effect on the villages on the Mediterranean coast.' How far do you agree with this statement? Explain your answer.

THE BRITISH HOLIDAY FIGHT-BACK

From the 1980s, the traditional British holiday resorts had to fight to survive in the face of competition from abroad. Some places such as Blackpool or Torquay remained consistently popular, while others such as Rhyl or Skegness struggled to attract tourists in the numbers they did up to the 1970s. The tourist industry in the UK had to adapt to social change and new interests in order to survive.

Updating traditional resorts

Ironically, the holiday camps suffered greatly from the cheap package deals that they had pioneered. They also suffered from an outdated public image, which gradually saw holiday camps as old-fashioned. By the 1980s they were only attracting half as many holidaymakers as they had in 1950. Butlin's re-branded itself in the 1980s, dropping its Hi-de-hi image in favour of 'themed worlds' such as Somerwest World in Minehead or Starcoast World in Pwllheli. Many well known camps have since had to close but others have continued to thrive, capitalising on the UK holidaymaker's love of the holiday camp.

Realising that many people still like the idea of a 'holiday camp', more up-market versions have sprung up, such as **Center Parcs** or Bluestone in Pembrokeshire. Rather than trying to compete with beach holidays abroad, these concentrate on activities that aren't affected so much by the British weather, such as indoor water complexes and outdoor activities.

A publicity photograph of Rhyl Sun Centre

Seaside resorts built large **leisure complexes** such as Swansea Leisure Centre and Rhyl Sun Centre, with indoor beaches, wave machines and tropical temperatures. In the 1990s, the Swansea centre was regularly featured in the top ten tourist destinations in Wales, attracting over 750,000 visitors a year.

Seaside resorts have had to clean up their environment, especially the water and the sand. Schemes like the Blue Flag awards have improved standards. Welsh beaches regularly win awards for cleanliness – in 2011, 41 beaches were awarded the coveted Blue Flag award.

Even the National Parks have had to adapt. Crowds of visitors flock to **'honey pot'** towns such as Windemere in the Lake District and the countryside remains a big draw for walkers, riders and devotees of outdoor pursuits. But more than any other attraction these beautiful areas have both benefited and suffered from tourism.

Llanddwyn beach on Anglesey, which regularly gains a Blue Flag award

Positive impacts of tourism on National Parks	Negative impacts of tourism on National Parks
1. Jobs and income for local people	1. Jobs are mainly seasonal, low paid with long hours
2. Increased demand for local food and crafts	2. Local goods can become expensive because tourists will pay more
3. Helps preserve rural services like buses, village shops, pubs and post offices	3. Demand for development of more shops and hotels
4. Tourists mainly come to see the scenery and wildlife helping to conserve habitats and wildlife	4. Damage to the landscape from litter, erosion, fires, traffic congestion and pollution
	5. Demand for holiday homes makes housing too expensive for local people

A balance sheet published by the National Parks Authority in its advice on sustainable tourism (2010)

New attractions

The period since the 1970s has also seen the tourist industry develop newer attractions to encourage people to spend time and money in the UK.

The first **theme park** in the UK opened at Thorpe Park in 1969. By 1992, total attendances at theme parks like Alton Towers, Drayton Manor and Oakwood had reached over 8 million. These parks competed with each other by adding more quality, excitement and originality to their rides.

The Corkscrew, Britain's first double loop roller coaster, opened at Alton Towers in 1980

Porthkerry Country Park near Barry

The continuing attraction of the countryside has seen many local authorities set up **country parks and nature trails**. Popular examples in Wales include Porthkerry Park near Barry and the Millennium coastal park at Llanelli. Farmers began to diversify, offering bed and breakfast and attractions on their land.

Many attractions have concentrated on using the past to ensure their future. Heritage – using history and historical sites to attract visitors – is becoming big business. There are many different types of historic attraction and open-air museums, such as St Fagans, Ironbridge and Beamish, and these have become particularly successful.

At Llancaiach Fawr in South Wales, guides dress up in 17th century costumes to entertain and inform tourists and visitors

Tourism in Cwm Rheidol, Mid Wales	
Pre 1930s	Occasional visits to Devil's Bridge: area still a lead-mining region, but in decline
1930s	Combined rail and charabanc trips on the Vale of Rheidol railway to see the scenery around Devil's Bridge
1960s	The Vale of Rheidol steam railway becomes a tourist attraction in itself after many lines close in Wales and England
1970s	Abandoned lead mines attract tourists interested in industrial archaeology
1990s	Back to nature: nature trails and woodland walks are set up and signposted
2000s	New attractions: visits to the hydro-electric power station and a 17 mile cycle trail

How tourism has developed in one area of Wales

TASKS

1. Make a list of the ways in which the British tourist industry has fought back against competition in recent years.

2. Survey your class. How many of them have experienced any of these types of attractions?

3. What does Source D tell you about indoor attractions in the UK?

4. Use Source B and your own knowledge to explain why holiday camps became less popular.

5. Create a balance sheet about whether you think the creation of National Parks has been positive or negative. Support your opinion with evidence that you have researched from the Internet.

6. Look at Source J. Make up a similar chart for a tourist area of your choice.

7. Discuss the following view: 'The British tourist industry cannot compete with the attractions of foreign countries.'

MODERN TRENDS IN HOLIDAY PATTERNS

So as the twenty-first century progresses, trends in holidays continue to change, but it is important to try and keep things in perspective. About 75% of holidays taken by British people are still spent in Britain and only a quarter are spent abroad. However foreign holidays usually last longer and cost more so the amount of money spent in the foreign resorts is considerably more. Evidence suggests that the percentage of people who do not go on long holidays remains the same as it did around 1970, but the number of people who can afford more than one holiday is increasing each year.

SOURCE A

Who comes with us?

They love music, football and DVDs. Cool bars and top clubs. Reading *The Sun*, *FHM*, *Heat*, *Nuts* and *ZOO*. They shop online. They live at home. They want to look good, feel good and don't care how much it costs. They drink Carling, Fosters, Stella, Bud, Corona, WKD, Smirnoff and Coca Cola. They work hard. They study hard. They live for the weekend. And by the summer, they're ready to leave it all behind

From a brochure for a holiday company aimed at selling holidays to young people (2010)

The key factors involved here are increased leisure time and increased income for many people. Other factors include competition between tourism firms, which keeps prices competitive and sophisticated advertising, which makes going on holiday now seem an essential part of people's lives. The rise of the Internet has meant that it is now easier to search for information about holiday destinations and to arrange holidays without leaving your home.

Holiday companies have begun to target specific groups beyond the traditional family unit. Firms like **Club 18-30** and resorts like Newquay in Cornwall have targeted the younger tourists, while others have offered special deals for the older holidaymakers.

SOURCE B

Older people need to realise there are many trips that meet their needs. Some 41 per cent of people aged over 55 will not be taking a summer break this year – which accounts for more than seven million Brits. People who often fit this bracket tend to have lost a partner or travelling companion and find it daunting to think of booking a holiday, as they are unsure of what to expect. Older people should look out for holidays with an itinerary of activities that they enjoy doing or that fit in with their special interests. Like-minded people are likely to be on the same sorts of trips.

Harold Burke, sales director at the charity Age Concern (2008)

Multi-holidays

Increasingly many people have more than one holiday a year. These include winter breaks abroad that offer exciting sports such as skiing and climbing. British resorts also try to attract people for short and weekend breaks.

SOURCE C

% of UK residents taking a holiday of over 4 nights duration			
Year	No holiday	1 holiday	More than 1 holiday
1971	41	44	15
1976	38	44	18
1981	39	40	20
1986	40	40	21
1991	40	36	24
1996	42	31	26
2001	41	30	29

Official figures compiled by the UK Tourist Agency

SOURCE D

A French ski resort

Would you rather have one big holiday, a couple of short breaks or lots of days out?

Question:
We have four children and just the thought of organising (and paying for!) a big holiday sends me into a cold sweat! Instead we tend to have a couple of short breaks, usually either camping or youth hostelling, often with a group of friends and then try to spend a few days with grandparents if we can and maybe fit in a couple of days out as well. What about you? Does it just not feel like a holiday unless you've had a couple of weeks on the beach or is a couple of days on a campsite enough to recharge your batteries?

Answer:
I tend to do both. I like to have a beach holiday somewhere hot and sunny, don't mind whether it's for one week or two as long as I get away somewhere. My daughter loves holiday camps, so I usually try to get a long weekend in there every year, and then we'll have a couple of camping weekends somewhere. Usually a site off peak, we can do that for less then a tenner a night, so they can be a pretty good break. But to answer your question I need both a longer holiday and a few short breaks.

A question and an answer from a website that provides advice for people (2010)

Environmental concerns

Another factor that has recently emerged, which has begun to have a bearing on people's holiday choice is the possible impact that travel has on the environment. This is especially connected with air travel. According to official figures, 54% of people claimed that they have become more concerned about the environmental impact of flying since 2005.

Airplane companies have been striving to create more fuel-efficient planes to reduce CO_2 emissions. The UK and other members of the EU have committed to reducing carbon emissions by 60% by 2050. Holidaymakers have been encouraged to consider changes in their habits to help solve the problem. In addition, the companies and businesses that provide accommodation and services for tourists have been encouraged to look at their businesses from an environmental perspective, tapping into the growing trend for eco-friendly holidays by using local food, reducing their **carbon footprint** and keeping their environmental impact to a minimum.

Neutralise the carbon emissions produced from your flight by donating towards conservation projects and the development of green energy. Avoid taking toiletries abroad in their packaging. Avoid driving all the way to the airport when you can park off-site and transfer to the airport terminal with everyone else. Buy food or souvenirs from local markets and businesses. Turn off lights, heating and air conditioning when you leave your hotel room. Conserve water by only putting your hotel towels out to be washed when they need it.

From a list of tips to holiday makers from a travel agency (2010)

When we arrived here in 2002, there had been no input to its structure since the end of World War I. Rats and cockroaches ran amok and there was not much of a roof. We had to pick it up and make it viable. We embraced green technology to make it sustainable. The house is now heated by a 150 kw biomass boiler and we have solar heating. We burn our own woodchips and we have since saved 66 tonnes of carbon, compared to oil. Sheep wool is used as insulation and we have a rainwater harvesting system. Food grown in our walled garden is sold through our farmers' shop and to local restaurants and we only use local produce which has traceability. Recycling is very important. It never ceases to amaze me as an accommodation provider, how much waste guests leave behind.

Gavin Hogg, owner of Penpont Hotel in Powys, interviewed in a tourist magazine (2008)

1. List five modern trends in holiday patterns.

2. Describe how the Internet has had an impact on tourism.

3. Use Sources A and B to explain why holidays are often targeted at different age groups.

4. How useful is Source C to an historian studying holiday patterns?

5. Answer the question posed in Source E for yourself.

6. Describe the environmental concerns that are now connected with holidays.

7. Explain how holidaymakers and tourist operators can help tackle environmental issues.

8. Discuss the following view: 'The most important influence on tourism since the 1970s has been the growth of package holidays.'

Here is an opportunity for you to practice some of the questions that have been explained in previous chapters.

These examples are taken from Section A of the examination and form an enquiry into changes in holiday patterns and trends. The questions test your source evaluation skills and are worth 25 marks in total.

Question 1(a) – comprehension of a visual source

SOURCE A

A photograph of a day out at the seaside in 1900

(a) What does Source A show you about traditional seaside resorts in 1900? [2]

- *Remember to pick out at least two facts from the picture;*
- *You can also make use of the information provided in the caption;*
- *For further guidance, see page 15.*

SOURCE B

A photograph taken at Butlin's in Skegness in the 1950s

(b) Use the information in Source B and your own knowledge to explain why Butlin's holiday camps were popular.

[4]

- *You will need to pick out at least two facts from the source and explain them in your own words;*
- *You must demonstrate your knowledge of this topic by providing at least one additional factor not mentioned in the source;*
- *For further guidance, see page 29.*

Question 1(c) – extent of support for a viewpoint

SOURCE C

Lots of families started to take their holidays abroad in the 1970s. Air travel became much more affordable and much more available. The older British seaside resorts such as Barry and Morecambe just couldn't offer the same for the holidaymakers.

From an article on tourism in the Western Mail *newspaper, 2007*

(c) How far does Source C support the view that the decline of British seaside resorts was due to cheap foreign holidays?

[5]

- *You must pick out a range of factors from both the source and the caption, linking them to your own knowledge;*
- *Remember to give a reasoned judgement that targets the question;*
- *For further guidance, see page 50.*

SOURCE D

> Every year we went to Rhyl on the train. But in 1959 when I was about 10, my uncle got a car. That year we went to Conwy Morfa for the weekend in the car! We'd never been there before because it was too far to walk from the station. No amusements, but sand dunes and an old quarry and a beach with no one else on it. I felt like I owned the place!

Alan Jones from Wrexham, remembering his childhood holidays in north Wales in an interview for a local newspaper (1999)

(d)   How useful is Source D to an historian studying changes in British holidays in the 1950s?

[6]

- *Aim to concentrate upon three focus areas – content, origin and purpose;*
- *Remember to make reference to the usefulness of the source to the historian;*
- *For further guidance, see page 64.*

SOURCE E

> I love visiting west Wales. My family has been coming here for many years. I don't see why people have to go abroad when there are such beautiful places to stay in and to visit. We are always spoiled for choice when it comes to activities, in good or bad weather. We like to walk on the coastal paths while the children have always loved playing on the beach and in the sea.

A mother of a growing family, giving an interview for a Welsh Tourist Board brochure (2001)

SOURCE F

> British holiday habits have changed considerably over the years. In the 1970s, the airline industry expanded and tour operators started to offer cheap packages to Spain. By the 1980s British tourists started to prefer a package holiday abroad rather than spend their holidays in Britain. By 2000 more and more people took two holidays abroad each year.

Pat Yale, a travel writer, writing in a textbook on leisure and tourism, Tourism in the UK (2002)

(e)   Why do Sources E and F have different views about holidays taken by British people?

[8]

- *You must comment upon both sources, in each case making reference to the content and the author;*
- *Remember to explain why the two sources have different views;*
- *For further guidance, see page 81.*

Glossary

Aerobatic displays	an attraction involving air displays and manoeuvres
Air travel	the opportunity for people to travel abroad by aeroplane
All-seater stadiums	sports grounds where spectators sit down and don't stand
Amateur sport	sport played as a pastime, not for money
Back to square one	a sporting catchphrase based on radio coverage of football matches
Bank Holiday Act	a law of 1871, which guaranteed people public holidays
Bank holidays	public holidays for workers granted by law
Bed and breakfast	a type of holiday offering accommodation and breakfast only
Beeching Axe	the closing of many railways in the 1960s
Bioscopes	an early way of watching moving films
Boarding house	a house where holiday-makers could rent rooms
Boycott	a refusal to take part in an event
Britpop	a British musical style of the 1990s
Broken-time	dispute over whether people should be paid if they took time off work to play sport
Caravan sites	areas for basing both touring and static caravans
Carbon footprint	the amount of carbon emissions created by people
CD players	a way of listening to music on compact discs
Center Parcs	a type of self-contained resort focused on family activities
Charabanc	a type of early coach, at first horse-drawn, later motorised
Club 18-30	holiday company that provides package holidays aimed at young adults
Commentators	people who talk about and describe sport on radio and television
Commercial television	television that is funded by advertisements
Cool Cymru	a nickname for the Welsh music scene of the 1990s
Country parks and nature trails	facilities available to encourage people to visit the countryside
Cymanfa ganu	a hymn singing festival
Derby match	a game played between teams from neighbouring places
European tour	a type of touring holiday undertaken mainly by richer people
Fictional sports stars	sports people who appeared in comics, books and films
Fighting booth	a fairground attraction that allowed people to box against each other
Football pools	a way of gambling by predicting the results of football matches
Girl Power	a nickname for the popularity of female pop groups in the late 1990s
Glam rock	a musical style of the 1970s, based on outrageous costumes
Holiday camp	a type of holiday offering accommodation, meals and entertainment on one site
Home computers	computers for personal use at home
Honey pot	a tourist destination that attracts large numbers of people
Household names	sports or media stars who are well known
Indoor sports centres	sporting facilities that are undercover
Jukeboxes	machines that played records, often in cafes and pubs
Leisure complexes	indoor facilities that contain a range of entertainment for visitors
Leisure time	free time for people
Live Aid	a charity campaign featuring famous musical artistes
Marketing	organized publicity for sporting events and players
Mass tourism	the tendency that large numbers of people will go away at the same time and to the same place

Matinées	afternoon performances in a cinema or theatre
Medal ceremony	way of rewarding athletes for their success in a competition
Miners' week	an annual paid holiday for industrial workers in south Wales
Ministry of Information	the government organization that controlled information during the Second World War
Minority sports	sports that don't often feature on television or in newspapers
Motels	hotels built to cater for motorists
MP3 players	a way of listening to music using digital audio files
Multi-screen cinemas	cinemas featuring several screens in one building
National parks	areas of great beauty protected by law
Newsreel	film of various events, including sports, shown in cinemas
Obesity 'epidemic'	the tendency for many people to be overweight
Outside broadcasts	radio and television broadcasts transmitted from the actual events, not from a studio
Package holidays	holidays where one payment covers accommodation, air transport and often meals, offered by a tour company
Paid holidays	a benefit for workers that became common from the 1920s
Paralympic Games	an organized international tournament for physically disabled athletes
Performance enhancing drugs	illegal substances used to improve sporting performance
Pierrots	clowns or comic singers that would perform at seaside resorts
Private gyms	sporting facilities that people pay a membership fee to use
Professional sport	sport played to earn money
Propaganda	the use of information to encourage people to think and behave in a certain way
Punk rock	an anti-establishment music style of the late 1970s
Record players	a way of listening to music on vinyl records
Rock'n'roll	a fast, loud musical style of the late 1950s
Rugby league	a form of rugby that was always professional
S4C	the Welsh language television channel
Satellite and cable channels	television service paid for by subscription
Seaside resort	a place where people would go to enjoy holidays by the sea
Skiffle	a simple musical style of the early 1960s
Social class	section of society, often based on background and/or income
Social networking	ways of communicating with others using the Internet
Spa towns	inland resorts that attracted tourists for the perceived health benefit of their mineral water
Special results edition	a newspaper containing the latest football scores, rushed out on Saturday evenings
Sponsorship	financial support for sports by businesses, often a form of advertising
Talent shows	television programmes that gave opportunities to new acts
Talkies	a nickname for films featuring sound
Teenybopper	a young music fan, associated with the 1970s
Temperance movement	a movement that campaigned against the drinking of alcohol
The Youth Hostel Association	an organization set up to provide cheap accommodation in rural areas
Theme park	an attractions that focuses on exciting rides and events
Tourist	a person that goes travelling for pleasure or on holiday
Triple Crown	an unofficial international rugby union competition between the nations of Britain
Wakes week	an annual paid holiday for industrial workers in north-west England
Walkman	a way of listening to music on cassettes